"Don Ross & Joshua Ziefle's new book, *A Tale of Two Churches* opens a great dialogue among those with a Pentecostal church legacy and a generation that's being engrafted into this wonderful biblical experience. The book finds balance so needed by these two generations and approaches it with a thoroughly scriptural and keen experiential insight. I'd encourage those who want to promote the church's Pentecostal DNA for a new generation to pick this book up for yourself and those you want to help in this journey."

— Ken Draughon, Superintendent, Alabama District Council

"Dr. Don Ross and Dr. Joshua Ziefle are urging the Church to a holistic theology whereby we combine the Lightning of the mission of Jesus with the Thunder of the power of the Spirit. Regardless of the tradition, denomination or tribe you identify with, it is incumbent upon us all to seek a deeper experience with the Spirit of God who is the greatest gift and our most vital resource for 21st Century ministry."

— Bruce D. Rhodes, Superintendent Southern Michigan, Free Methodist Church

"One of the most misunderstood theological topics centers around the phenomenon of speaking in an unknown language, especially within a worship services. Ross and Ziefel launched into the topic with great clarity and no hesitation to discuss the importance of living a Spirit filled life. They combine the history of Pentecost with a theological understanding for why the Holy Spirit is necessary for effective ministry and witness, along with practical stories from their own experience and clear steps forward."

— Dave E. Cole, D. Min, Assistant Superintendent at the Northwest Ministry Network, Author of *Re-Focus: Creating An Outward-Focused Church Culture*

"*A Tale of Two Churches* gives a voice to the thoughts and inner struggles of many pastors who care about what their church needs to be and do. The transparency of the personal stories of the authors and the historical and biblical expositions convincingly point to the fact that the Holy Spirit is actively involved in the being and the doing of the church. This Pentecostal theology is supposed to be our pastoral theology. There is a bridge between the evangelistic Acts and the pastoral 1 Corinthians, and the reader is offered a lot to reflect and decide on from the panoramic view of this bridge."

— Joseph Dimitrov, Ph.D., President, Continental Theological Seminary, Brussels, Belgium; Chairman, World Assemblies of God Fellowship Theological Commission

"This book had to be written! The question being posed in this book is, 'How can a Pentecostal not be missional?' While many have embraced the Spirit and His gifts, they have never embraced the Spirit's empowering for the mission of the gospel. Ross and Ziefle call us out on this fact, and show us Acts as a model for going forward. They highlight the balance between the gospel mission and Holy Spirit empowerment. Being missional doesn't mean compromising or watering down Christ's mission command and being empowered by the Spirit doesn't mean being extreme or ultra conservative. This is a focused, practical and compelling read."

— Dr. Greg Mundis, Assemblies of God World Missions Director

"This is a great book! *A Tale of Two Churches* speaks to the issue at the heart of our current struggle. The challenge of growing churches that are both missionally effective and yet functionally Pentecostal is frequently like the elephant in the room. That is what makes this such an important read. Here is a theological, practical and integrated approach to an issue that is central to our mission in the world."

— James T. Bradford, General Secretary, The General Council of the Assemblies of God, Author of *Lead So Others Can Follow*

"If we're honest, it's a theological and spiritual quandary with which many of us who call ourselves Pentecostal have wrestled: how is it possible to be fully Pentecostal and fully 'missional' in a way that is authentic to both? And what in the world would that look like? In *A Tale of Two Churches: Why Being Both Missional and Pentecostal Matters*, Drs. Donald Ross and Joshua Ziefle turn that question on its head: how is it possible to NOT be fully Pentecostal and fully missional in a way that is authentic to both? The answer is good news for honest hearts longing to thrive in the fullness of the Spirit while living out the gospel in a way that compels others to come to Jesus. Offering a rich theological and historical context coupled with relatable personal stories and the kind of wise insights that come only from years of walking with God, *A Tale of Two Churches* shows us it is not only possible to be 'missionally-Pentecostal' (or 'Pentecostally-missional'), it is precisely what God had in mind all along...and exactly what this waiting world needs."

— Dr. Jodi Detrick, Former Seattle Times columnist,
Author of *The Jesus-Hearted Woman*

"*A Tale of Two Churches* provides a much-needed resource for pastors and church leaders in the 21st century who want to develop a church both vibrant in Holy Spirit empowerment and effective in reaching the lost. Breaking down the barriers dividing 'Pentecostal' and 'Missional' labels, my friends Don Ross and Joshua Ziefle merge the views of a practitioner and a scholar to focus on what is truly important. Their historical review and personal stories provide a foundation based on sound biblical and theological research. Next, they provide clear guidance upon which to build concrete next steps in any ministry context. These practical steps make it possible to experience the Spirit's power in a fresh way for effective ministry in our day."

— Don Detrick, D.Min., Associate Network Leader,
Northwest Ministry Network and Adjunct Professor,
Northwest University and Assemblies of God Theological
Seminary, Author of *Growing Organic Disciples*

"If we want to build healthy Pentecostal churches, we should model them on the churches in the Book of Acts, not the church of Corinth. Acts shows us powerful Spirit-filled churches in motion, in mission. The Corinthian letters focus on correcting a church side-tracked by emotion and error. Ross & Ziefle explore this contrast to help us respond to the purpose of the Corinthian letters—returning them to the missional model of the Apostolic churches."

> — Joseph Castleberry, Ed.D., President, Northwest University, Author of *The New Pilgrims: How Immigrants are Renewing America's Faith and Values*

"Don Ross and Joshua Ziefle put their finger on a sore-spot in the Pentecostal community, especially in this day of increasing church declines. They are mission-first leaders who adeptly challenge the assumption that a fiery Pentecostal expression will automatically equate to effective evangelism, and gives an alternate way to hold the precious moving of the Spirit."

> — Verlon Fosner, D. Min, Author of *Dinner Church: Building Bridges by Breaking Bread*

"Dr. Donald E. Ross and Dr. Joshua Ziefle have written an excellent book! *A Tale of Two Churches* eloquently explains the transition of the Pentecostal Church over the past years. This book should be read by every Pastor who has experienced frustration or questioned when revival is coming to the church. You cannot separate the work of the Holy Spirit and the Mission of the Church. Pastor, this is a definite must read!"

> — Gilbert Daniel Olivarez, Superintendent Central District/Distrito Central

"The message of *A Tale of Two Churches*... is very overdue! Don and Joshua humbly share their personal journeys that relate to many questions I have had. Why do some churches gravitate toward only a Sunday Spirit-filled experience? Why do other Pentecostal churches seem willing to sacrifice their Spirit-filled expression or dependence so they can avoid offending seekers? This book clearly argues that tension and confusion between Missional and Pentecostal emphasis need not exist! Reaching our world for Jesus should not steer clear of the gifts of the Holy Spirit. Service and evangelism should be the natural expression of the presence and power of the Holy Spirit; even utterly dependent. This book articulates how the mission is paramount and how the Spirit empowers its success."

— Alan Schaberg, Superintendent, Wyoming Ministry Network

"Like Ross and Ziefle, I've encountered the duality of style in Pentecostal ministry—spiritual weirdness (odd manifestations and insider holiness traditions) as proof of orthodox Pentecostalism vs. 'toned-down' attractional church services where non-Pentecostals and the unchurched can feel welcome. The authors encourage us to embrace an integrated model of leadership, training our congregations in sound biblical theology and practice, and then sending people into their communities, empowered by the Holy Spirit for the mission of God."

— Rosemarie Daher Kowalski, Ph. D., Church Planter,
Author of *When the Spirit Said Go*

"I was born in the fire and I can't live in the smoke. To many churches are living in the smoke rather than the fire. God has a plan for your church to be on fire. My friends Dr. Joshua Ziefle and Dr. Don Ross have tremendous insights about leading a church that is both on mission and on fire."

— Bill Wilson, Network Lead Pastor,
Oregon Ministry Network of the Assemblies of God

"Northwest Assemblies of God Network Superintendent, Dr. Don Ross and Princeton-trained, Northwest University professor, Dr. Joshua Ziefle have provided a gem for today's church and her leaders. Genuine practitioners, they've demonstrated empowerment of pneumatocentric mission; contextualized Pentecostal Missional Ecclesiology. It's a stirring read with revival insights from 1801's-Cane Ridge, Ky, to LA's Bonnie Brae Street meetings and Azusa revival of 1906, to their own church stories of today and more. Yes!, The twin-theme of Missional and Pentecostal naturally belong together."

— Dr. Joseph S. Girdler, Superintendent, Kentucky Ministry
  Network, Assemblies of God

"Drs. Don Ross and Joshua Ziefle invite pastors, missionaries and church leaders to join them in their journey of discovery of the church being fully Pentecostal and fully missional. From their unique perspectives of pastor, network leader and university professor, they provide an accurate historical context of churches being missional while also being empowered by the Holy Spirit. They wrestled with the current and future direction of the church, challenging the readers to examine the issue for themselves. Anyone concerned about a de-emphasis on being Pentecostal owes it to themselves to read this book."

— Barbara D. Petty, Ph.D., Chair,
  Northwest University Board of Directors

"I appreciate Don Ross and Joshua Ziefle honestly tackling this significant and emotion-packed issue. *A Tale of Two Churches* is a gift to Spirit-filled local church leaders who are pursuing the biblical mission of advancing God's kingdom. This book facilitates a strategic discussion that could result in the spiritual renewal of your church and your community."

— Tom Jacobs, Superintendent, Iowa Ministry Network,
  Assemblies of God

"*A Tale of Two Churches* is a must read for every Pentecostal leader and for the people they lead. It really helped me deal with the 'Pentecostal / Missional' tension in my own life. Dr. Ross and Dr. Ziefle address the stress between being Pentecostal and being Missional that often divides our churches and show how and why it is not either or but both that make up an Acts 2 church."

— Alan Warneke, Superintendent, Montana Ministry Network, Assemblies of God

"Don Ross and I have developed a growing friendship around a common passion. We want to see the power of God at work in the churches we serve and love. Our traditions are rooted in the Wesleyan idea that the Holy Spirit was given at Pentecost to empower the church and enable the believer to live a life marked by victory and love. While I would not put the emphasis where Don does, the question remains the same, 'Did you received the Holy Spirit when you believed?' Like sail boats on a calm day, without the blowing breeze of the Spirit, our churches are dead in the water no matter how fine their rigging."

— Jerry Kester, District Superintendent, Washington Pacific District Church of the Nazarene

"A Pentecost that does not produce disciples for Christ is a Pseudo–Pentecost! In *A Tale of Two Churches*, Don and Joshua take us to the heart of our challenge and concern, and present us with an understanding of our history and a biblically sound exegesis of a model for our consideration. I am ready for a New Wine Skin!"

— Robert Wise, Jr., Pastor/Superintendent, Southern New England Ministry Network

A TALE OF
TWO CHURCHES

A TALE OF
TWO CHURCHES

WHY BEING BOTH MISSIONAL
& PENTECOSTAL MATTERS

DONALD E. ROSS & JOSHUA ZIEFLE

3RD EDITION

TURNAROUND CHURCH
COACHING NETWORK

Turnaround Church Coaching Network
6163 NE 194th Place
Kenmore, WA 98028

Printed in the United States of America
1 2 3 4 5 6 7 8 9 10
ISBN: 978-0-9897698-7-7

DEDICATION

THIS BOOK IS DEDICATED to the pastors, missionaries, and church leaders in the Northwest Ministry Network with whom we are privileged to serve. Nearly 1,400 of you, who are called by God, reach out to the seven million people within the geographical boundaries of our Network.

You serve from the Pacific Ocean to the Montana border and from the Canadian border to the Oregon border. You lead nearly 350 churches and serve as missionaries in nearly sixty countries around the world. Thank you for giving your lives away, one day at a time, for the gospel of Jesus.

Each one of you has dedicated your life to our Network's mission, "Bringing the Hope of Jesus to our Communities." Your sacrifice and commitment not only honor the call of Jesus on your life, but they also honor those you serve in the communities in which you live.

We know without the Holy Spirit's power, we will never be able to reach out effectively to the six million residents in our region who have not embraced the gospel of Jesus, so this book is dedicated to you, it is written for you, and hopefully it will be an encouragement to you. May God give you grace to fully live out the calling on your lives, empowered by his Spirit to move the mission of Jesus forward.

Sincerely,
Dr. Donald E. Ross
Dr. Joshua Ziefle

CONTENTS

FOREWORD

IS IT POSSIBLE for the Church to be Pentecostal and missional at the same time? Acts 2 gives a clear answer of "Yes!" These two qualities were intertwined, seemingly inseparable pieces of the birth of the Church.

Was that event only for the apostolic era, not to be repeated? Acts reports the early story of the Church, and clearly shows that the Spirit-empowered church was missional. The Church did not cease being Pentecostal, nor did it cease being missional. The summary given in Acts 2:42-47 makes it clear that the exercise of spiritual gifts continued, and that the Church continued in her growth.

Persecution didn't stop God's activity: the number of believers increased (Acts 4:4). Following the Sanhedrin's attempt to rein in this upstart group, the disciples met together. "After they prayed, the place where they were meeting was shaken. And they were all filled with the Holy Spirit and spoke the word of God boldly." (Acts 4:31 – NIV) The growth continued (5:14; 6:7). Then came the first martyr: Stephen (Acts 7). Greater persecution followed, and the believers were scattered. This only had the effect of spreading the activity of the Spirit further, and more believed (8:4-8). Saul entered the scene, first as an enemy of the Church, and then as one who encountered Christ and now spoke for him.

One result of Saul's conversion was a time of relative peace. "Then the church throughout Judea, Galilee and Samaria enjoyed a time of peace and was strengthened. Living in the fear of the Lord and encouraged by the Holy Spirit, it increased in numbers." Neither persecution nor peace stopped the growth of the Spirit-empowered Church. The ongoing story in Acts is well worth reading!

Can the churches of today be true to this birthright? Don Ross and Joshua Ziefle ask the important question: Why does it seem that so many Pentecostal churches today are not missional, and why are many missional churches not operating fully in the Spirit, even though they bear a Pentecostal label? The early Church was clearly both Pentecostal and missional.

Ross and Ziefle propose a way forward, returning to the roots seen in Acts 2. Don Ross has been my pastor for many years, first as lead pastor at The Creekside Church in North Seattle, and now as the Network Leader (Superintendent) of the Northwest Ministry Network of the Assemblies of God. With a rich Pentecostal ancestry, Ross has seen church growth and decline, and has been instrumental in the "Turnaround Church" movement.

Joshua Ziefle has been a colleague at Northwest University, serving as Associate Professor of Youth Ministries. His PhD is in American Church History, focusing on David du Plessis and the interaction between the Charismatic Movement and the Assemblies of God. Ross and Ziefle bring practical experience, research, and theoretical knowledge to the discussion.

The only possible answer to the question of "Can the churches of today be both Pentecostal and missional?" is that they MUST be both. The Great Commission was not given in a void, with hopes that something would happen. The One who called us did so with the promise to send the Holy Spirit to empower us. That promise was fulfilled on the day of Pentecost, but as Peter exhorted that first audience, "Repent and be baptized, every one of you, in the name of Jesus Christ for the forgiveness of your sins. And you will receive the gift of the Holy Spirit. The promise is for you and your children and for all who are far off—for all whom the Lord our God will call." (Acts 2:38-39)

The promise is for us all. It includes the gift of the Holy Spirit, but the mention of those whom "God will call" also brings a promise of growth in God's kingdom. Ross and Ziefle call us back to our roots: to the reality of the Spirit-empowered Pentecostal church which is fully engaged in her mission.

— Waldemar Kowalski, Ph.D. NT Theology, University of Gloucestershire, UK, Professor of Bible & Theology, Northwest University, Member of the Theology Commission of the Assemblies of God

INTRODUCTION

THIS BOOK IS THE STORY OF TWO CHURCHES, but let me share a little bit of my story first.

In the fall of 2014, my world changed significantly. After many years as the lead pastor in a local church, I was selected to lead the Northwest Ministry Network, comprised of over 300 churches and 1,400 ministers. It was a new day for my wife Brenda and me.

Previous to this leadership role, I led Creekside Church, located just north of Seattle, Washington, for twenty years. I tell the whole story (the good, bad, and ugly) in my book, *Turnaround Pastor*. The church hit a high of 2,000 in attendance and then plummeted downward due to a variety of leadership issues. I joined the leadership team as lead pastor at the 350 level, then endured the ride down to 150, where we remained stuck for nearly five years. It was not a fun ride.

During the plateaued years of 2004-2009, we purchased property and relocated, survived the national financial crisis, and made $25,000 monthly payments on our mortgage. How we survived as a church is a tribute to Jesus' faithfulness, but this adventure clearly prepared me for the new role as Network Leader that I was being asked to take.

Within a few months of becoming its leader, the Northwest Ministry Network launched one of the most aggressive initiatives in our denominational history. We proposed to plant one hundred new churches in Washington and northern Idaho in three years. I knew Jesus was asking me to lead this initiative, and I also knew a simple, mission-focused, regional strategy was not enough to give us the cultural traction we needed to be successful.

I knew we needed the power of the Holy Spirit to accomplish this gargantuan goal, but I also knew I was conflicted internally on the very topic of the Holy Spirit. It was not that I doubted our doctrine on the Holy Spirit or the Spirit-empowered baptism taught in the Scriptures. I fully embraced both of those. Rather, my conflictions had to do with local church life and the Holy Spirit. Now for the story of two churches.

Imagine this first church is a focused, historic, Pentecostal church, with Pentecostal applications in ministry. The gifts of the Spirit are active in nearly every worship service. Worshipers are impacted emotionally, as well as spiritually. Tongues, prophecy, and singing in the Spirit are commonplace. From time to time, people are healed, or they even fall to the floor, which is called "slain in the Spirit." A deep sense of God's presence is felt as the church is gathered together.

From time to time, this church may go a little extreme by some standards, with some loud wailing or emotional outburst that seems to detract, but everyone in this church seems to take it in stride. People come forward for an "altar service" at the end of almost every service to pray or respond to God's call in their lives. The obvious reason for gathering is to be together with one another and to sense God in their midst. For those purposes, it is "mission accomplished" in this church.

However, something is missing. Many in the church feel it, but very few are willing to talk about it.

It has been some time since any new believers have come to Christ. Adult baptisms are rare, and very few stories are told of people talking about Jesus with those outside the church. The church's mission to reach the lost is known, but it does not really affect the church's operation. In a sense, this Pentecostal experience has been compartmentalized and relegated to Sunday church services only.

It is as though the mission of this church is more about feeling God's presence than sharing God's presence with others outside the church. While sensing God in our lives is always good, sharing the gospel is mission critical. The good news is we do not have to choose between the two, but in a way, this church has chosen the former over the latter. They are experience rich and mission poor.

In a line, it could be said this church is Pentecostal but not missional.

Enter the second church, which also has a historic, Pentecostal foundation, but the Pentecostal application during worship is significantly different than the first church. Worship is lively, new people are often present in the worship services, and the language from the stage reflects the consideration that not everyone in the room understands all that is happening. Explanations about songs, communion, Scripture, and other service aspects are frequent and appreciated.

This church offers baptisms for new believers on a regular basis and classes for new believers to the Christian faith. At the end of nearly every service, some kind of response is encouraged, but rarely are people asked to come forward. It is clear this church does not want to embarrass or offend those exploring faith in Christ. All in all, this church seems to be very focused on the mission of Jesus to reach lost people.

Again, something is missing. Many in the church feel it, but very few are willing to talk about it.

Older believers remember the days when the power of the Spirit was more deeply present in worship services, and they long to experience that again. Nevertheless, they are excited about seeing new believers in their church, but conversations about living a Spirit-empowered life rarely involve discussing any of the Spirit's gifts, especially speaking in tongues.

In a line, it could be said this church is missional but not Pentecostal.

These two churches represent a growing frustration in Pentecostal leaders. The frustration is that if a church is fully Pentecostal, it cannot be effectively missional in winning the lost, and if it is fully missional, it cannot be effectively Pentecostal. I understand the agonizing dichotomy presented by these two churches, because I have pastored both. This is the conflict.

I was able to keep quiet inside me for a long time, but it was becoming an ecclesiastical nausea within me. Within a short time, this would no longer be inside, or quiet.

Enter Dr. Joshua Ziefle.

I am not saying Josh made me sick, in fact, far from it. I am saying God connected us during this season of frustration.

I met Josh for the first time at the home of Dr. Joseph Castleberry, President of Northwest University. Joe hosted "pizza theology" nights for board members, and Josh was the featured speaker. He spoke on the Holy Spirit, specifically on his doctoral dissertation on David du Plessis, who was an apostle of the Holy Spirit to the ecumenical movement from the 1950s to 1970s.

Following his presentation, he opened the session for questions. I had been in my new leadership role for two weeks at this point, but I had to ask my question. I knew the moment I asked this question, I would be bracketed theologically. Nevertheless, I was compelled. I raised my hand, was recognized, and launched into my query.

"Dr. Ziefle," I began, "my question has to do with the mission of the church and the Holy Spirit in operation in the local church. My experience as a lead pastor for thirty years took me through several chapters. I was raised in Pentecostal expression with the voice gifts being manifested weekly in our services. We classified a good service as having a prophecy or message in tongues with interpretation. A lackluster service did not, but I began to notice a shift in my first church. People became reluctant to invite their friends to church, and when they did, they gave disclaimers about the service."

At this point, the room was very quiet. Hardly anyone knew me, and they all wanted to see where I was going with this. I knew I had one foot in the rowboat and one on the dock, and I had to keep going, setting the stage for my question.

"My members would tell their friends things may happen in the service that would seem strange to them, maybe even a little weird, but they should not be put off by them. Everything would be fine. By the time the explanation was over, the new person was basically talked out of coming to church. It was frustrating to watch."

I continued, "I began to seek out what it meant to be an out-ward-focused or a missional church, because I wanted to see people come to Christ. There were two primary missional champions at the time—Bill Hybels from Willow Creek Church and Rick Warren from Saddleback Church—and neither of these churches were Pentecostal. I was very impressed with their focus on the mission of Jesus to reach lost people, and this was, in fact, the first time I heard the word 'missional' used in the local church context.

"In short, as our church became more missional by focusing on reaching lost people, we became less Pentecostal, at least in the way I had historically experienced it. People were coming to Christ now, and that was exciting, but it seemed like we weren't as empowered as we should be. I know the Holy Spirit was helping us, because no one can come to Christ without the work of the Holy Spirit, but I was not satisfied with that answer."

It was like I was more Binarian than Trinitarian in function.

I continued the lead up to my question. "It was like Acts 1:8, 'But you will receive power when the Holy Spirit comes on you; and you will be my witnesses in Jerusalem, and in all Judea and Samaria, and to the ends of the earth' was in conflict with Acts 2:4, 'All of them were filled with the Holy Spirit and began to speak in other tongues as the Spirit enabled them.' We know the Holy Spirit was given to us to empower us to be witnesses, but it seems the exact opposite is happening."

Now was the time for me to pop the question. I had set the stage. I had ignored my inner fears and possible rejection by my peers and plunged ahead in an effort to deal with my own internal conflicts.

Finally, I asked, "Dr. Ziefle, in light of what I have just described, can you help me understand how we can be both missional in reaching lost people and Pentecostal, empowered by the Holy Spirit, at the same time?"

I will never forget his answer. He looked at me and said, "Hmmm… I'm not sure I have a good answer to your question, but I do understand your frustration. I don't think you are alone."

I appreciated Josh's honesty, and I sensed he could potentially be someone with whom I could process. Even though we are decades apart in age, it seemed like God was connecting us.

About six months later, I was asked to speak at a conference at which Josh was also speaking, and we found ourselves at breakfast together in the same hotel. We picked up this same conversation on the tension between a church being missional and a church being historically Pentecostal. We sensed the Holy Spirit wanted to connect us, as we were both clearly energized by this topic.

We began to record our conversation, which turned into the raw material for an article, which eventually turned into this book. We explored a simple question: if the Holy Spirit was sent by Jesus to empower the church to be effective in the mission of reaching lost people, how can we be both missional and Pentecostal?

If you are a pastor, this book is for you, because it is impossible to do God's will in your own power. If you are a church lay leader, this book is for you, because you are on the front lines of ministry. If you are a follower of Jesus with no official leadership responsibility, then you hold a most critical position as a frontline member of Christ's army of compassion, committed to sharing the gospel with others.

It is clear God wants his church to be missional, focused on reaching lost people, and it is just as clear Jesus sent the Holy Spirit to empower us for this task. The rest of this book attempts to answer that question, and both Josh and I hope you will join us on the journey.

CHAPTER ONE
OUR STORIES

JOSH'S STORY

MY OWN JOURNEY to the "pizza theology" night at our university president's home was somewhat different than Don's, but the results have been no less important. To explain how I ended up in that particular moment, I hope you will indulge me in the opportunity to share a little background. I believe it has importance for the topic at hand.

Retrospect is interesting. Even at the relatively young age of 36, I am able to look back and see the many ways God has been at work in my life and circumstances that have helped bring me to this place and time. Unbelievably, all of it has actually led me to write this very book. My story of faith begins when I was in junior high.

Though I had not grown up in the church, my grandmother, visiting with us for a few months, saw fit to take me with her to Sunday services. The church in southern New Jersey was small—never more than around one hundred people—but powerful. A deep sense of community and joy was evident in that place. I was quickly welcomed into their youth ministry program. Before long, I was deeply involved.

Though I cannot point to a particular day that I can testify to becoming a Christian believer, I do know that during that short season of early adolescence, I began to come to an understanding of who Jesus was in my life. My whole experience of faith to that point—indeed, for a number of years afterwards, as well—was in that one church. I am thankful that it was such a healthy place to learn and grow.

However, I did not fully understand or appreciate at the time just one aspect of the congregation. It was not just any church; it was a Pentecostal church. The people in attendance believed strongly God's Holy Spirit was alive and active in extraordinary ways in their lives and in the midst of our church gatherings.

During times of worship through song, church members would speak in tongues, and interpretations would be given. Testimonies of God's provision and intervention were shared. Miracles and healings were discussed so often they seemed commonplace. Sunday nights nearly always featured extended times of prayer, and together around the altars we worshiped, interceded, and sought the move of the Spirit.

I know now the Pentecostal expression of the Christian faith is but one of a multitude of ways believers have embraced their faith over time and around the world. Back then, however, I had no such awareness. For me, being a Christian meant being like my church. Though the gifts of the Spirit expressed in a Sunday service were certainly different from other parts of my life, I mostly thought it was normal Christian experience. When I first spoke in tongues the month after returning from youth camp, I felt I had reached an important milestone in my life of faith. Everything felt different.

Pentecostals have a reputation for being anti-intellectual. Thankfully, my church was not one of these. I was always an academically interested student, and church members never hesitated to encourage me. Upon graduation from high school, I attended a Christian college. Though not affiliated with the Pentecostal movement, this solid evangelical institution helped ground me in the core teachings of the faith. I also developed more of my passion for the field of history (my major), while focusing a significant amount of attention on theological and biblical topics, as well.

During this season of life, I was away from my home church. I rarely, if ever, attended a Pentecostal congregation during my semesters at school. In the process, I encountered solid Christian believers of many different types. Though thankful for this broader vision of faith, this new exposure, combined with my intellectual pursuits, forced me to ask certain questions about my previously uncritical Pentecostal acceptance. Was it too emotional? Were Pentecostal services manipulative? Was our worship, as one friend called it in college, "Christian hedonism"? Was Pentecostalism a legitimate expression of faith?

As my time in college ended, and I began work on my master's degree at Princeton Seminary, these questions percolated in my brain. I asked myself difficult questions about whether or not Pentecostalism was real and whether or not it was where I belonged. I knew the truth of my experience, but the power we Pentecostals always talked about seemed lacking. I did not doubt Christ; I just doubted whether the work of the Holy Spirit as described in the book of Acts had anything to do with what happened in most Pentecostal churches. In my frustration, a moment came in which I almost left it behind.

Thankfully, God had other plans, which included a two-pronged approach. First, he directed me to a conference where I met Pentecostal believers who encouraged me with a deep passion for the work and reality of the Spirit I had not seen for years. Second, he led me to an unplanned church service in which I suddenly knew, beyond a shadow of a doubt, I was called to pastoral ministry in the Assemblies of God.

My return to seminary for my second and third years involved active service in a local Pentecostal church and a "doubling down" of my exploration of what it meant to be a Pentecostal believer. Added to this was the unique experience that was Princeton Seminary—an institution with a diverse theological and denominational student population.

I can still recall sitting in the school's cafeteria and being asked questions about my faith. Was I a Pentecostal? What was that like? Could I speak in tongues? Could I do it right now? I was, ready for it or not, a Pentecostal ambassador to a group of Presbyterians, Lutherans, Methodists, and others whose knowledge extended little beyond what they might have seen on the Internet or watched as they flipped through one of "those" television channels.

I quickly came to embrace my new role as a "token Pentecostal" at Princeton. I leaned into this reality not only in my personal interactions, but also through my academic work. By the time I moved on to the next phase of my scholarly studies, I decided I wanted to focus my doctoral work on the history of Pentecostalism.

Even then, though, God made sure I was grounded. In the very same season I began my PhD in church history, I also started serving as a youth pastor at my local Assemblies of God church. I would do both together for the next five and one-half years.

It took a little while, but eventually I settled upon the person who would be the subject of my dissertation: David du Plessis. As a Pentecostal minister in the middle of the twentieth century, du Plessis believed the Pentecostal work of the Holy Spirit was not meant to be fenced off within traditional Pentecostal denominations. It was meant for the whole church. The latter half of his life was spent as a missionary of the Spirit to other Christian denominations. They had the truth, of course, but it was "the truth on ice." He came to bring them "fire and the Holy Spirit."

As he and others worked during the midcentury, they were well placed to connect with the charismatic movement that was springing up around them. Presbyterians, Episcopalians, Roman Catholics, and others began to experience Pentecostal-style revivals in their own settings. They embraced divine healing, and they spoke in tongues. They were hungry for something more from God. As they received, people like du Plessis helped them understand, explain, and deepen their experience.

David du Plessis's role as a Pentecostal ambassador provided a natural way for me to connect with his life. My own time in seminary as one of the few representatives of Pentecostalism echoed his journey decades before. However, and this is important, my time as a youth pastor complicated this idealistic picture. For as much as I believed with du Plessis that the power of the Holy Spirit was important, it was not something I emphasized much in ministry.

Evangelism, community, and discipleship were my core themes. I wanted students to know Jesus, have a spiritual home, and grow in their knowledge of the faith. While I certainly believed in miracles, tongues, words of knowledge, and the deep and abiding work of the Holy Spirit, I decided I would not lead with those particulars. I did not want to scare people away with the weird stuff. After all, I thought, Jesus is more important. I, like many, reserved the Holy Spirit for a summer camp or winter retreat—in the process, farming it all out to the "professionals."

As much as I believed in and was inspired by the work of people like du Plessis, in my life as a pastor, I shied away from those areas in which he was so passionate. I had experienced the Holy Spirit in powerful ways, yet I was afraid of "rocking the boat" in youth ministry by being fully Pentecostal. The disconnect between belief and practice is something that was never resolved during my six years as a youth pastor.

The tension traveled with me, though, as I transitioned to my current role as a professor at Northwest University. Interacting daily with college students studying to be pastors—many of whom are from the Pentecostal/charismatic tradition—meant that I was constantly thinking about the best and most authentic ways to minister. Here in the Pacific Northwest, that often looks like embracing a lot of cutting-edge styles, techniques, and marketing. We want people to connect with Jesus in a biblical yet culturally relevant way, and our culture leads us to do this in ways that are sensitive to these needs.

Traditional Pentecostal characteristics often run at odds with this.

At the same time, I am a Pentecostal. I really believe in this. I have also continued my work as a Pentecostal historian. This means looking not just into American expressions of the movement, but also into the way in which the revival has developed and been embraced the world over. This latter part has been a particular challenge for me.

If you look at the Christian world today and throughout the past century, without a doubt, it has been the Pentecostal and charismatic movement that has shown the most energy, vigor, and growth. The numbers are astounding, and I will share about that later in this book. Not only that, but elsewhere around the world, believers have embraced the supernatural and extravagant gifts of the Holy Spirit. In places like Latin America, Africa, and Asia, it is arguably these same expressions of power and promises that God intervenes into our daily lives that have led to such growth.

When I look at Pentecostalism today in many part of the United States, though, this same emphasis on the Holy Spirit's unexpected work in our daily lives is often downplayed. Contemporary culture, we believe, dictates that we operate in other ways and remain more "dignified" than our Pentecostal ancestors or fellow believers around the world today.

At least, that is what we think.

These are some of the thoughts that began rolling around in my mind when our university president asked me to speak at the "pizza theology" night. It is intimidating for a junior professor to be asked to speak before the board of trustees, but when the president asks, you do not say no! I described to those gathered (Don included) some of what I have written here. I shared how outsiders' interest in the work of the Holy Spirit sparked the charismatic revival during the 1960s.

I pointed to how many of our sisters and brothers around the globe would be surprised how little we who call ourselves Pentecostals truly embrace the Holy Spirit's miraculous and unexpected work. I reflected on how we might embrace our faith not in name only, but also in reality. I wondered how we might take a seat and look to benefit from others around the world who have embraced the power of God. Then, borrowing from and adapting the words of German pastor Dietrich Bonhoeffer, I asked, simply, "Who is the Holy Spirit for us today?"

I believe that these questions are a part of my story. They are ones that God has been preparing me to ask. From those early days in the Pentecostal congregation of my youth, to my academic studies at Princeton, to my calling to minister and to teach ministry students, God has led me to a place where these reflections are natural extensions of my experience.

It was encouraging, then, that my new friend Don—experienced minister, pastor to pastors—was asking the very same questions. Though a full generation apart in age and experience, we are both sensing the same pull to a reevaluation of the way that twenty-first century Pentecostals live their faith. If the Holy Spirit is who we say, then it means changes need to be made. Even more than my story, Don's has led him to believe this powerfully. Now it is his turn to tell you how he got to that point.

DON'S STORY

I was born in Ballard, a community within Seattle. I grew up in a Pentecostal home while my parents were helping my grandfather, Ben Nelson, plant a church with the Open Bible denomination. It was a Pentecostal church, and my grandfather had deep Pentecostal roots; however, he was raised Lutheran, due to his Norwegian heritage.

I was raised in a fully Pentecostal heritage, but it did not begin that way. My mother was born with tuberculosis of the spine and given only six months to live. At the time, my grandfather was a Minnesota corn farmer, and when he was given his new baby daughter's diagnosis, he was desperate. He walked out into the cornfield, knelt, and prayed, asking a God he barely knew to heal his baby girl, who would later become my mother.

Even though his Lutheran family banned Pentecostals, he took my mother and his young wife to an Assemblies of God church, where they both independently made personal commitments to Christ. They asked the pastor to pray for my mother, and she went home healed. Grandpa Ben kept his word and ministered the gospel for seventy years, planting churches in Montana, Washington, and Florida. I was honored to preach his funeral when he died at age ninety.

My father was not raised Pentecostal. He lived in the small farming community of St. John, Washington, and came to Christ at age fifteen during revival meetings held at the local Assemblies of God church. Following the revival meeting one night, he headed home to tell his gospel-resistant parents that he had been called into ministry. He was formulating how to tell them this news, and he had no idea what was waiting for him.

Years before, during the Depression, my paternal grandfather, Tom Ross, was leading a group of families who became trapped by snow in the Idaho mountains. They were cutting wood to trade for food. No one was in danger, and they had plenty of supplies. However, since my father was a baby and required special food, my grandfather became worried, because they had run out of food for the infant.

My unbelieving grandfather walked out into the snow, much like my other grandfather had walked out into a cornfield, and he prayed. He asked a God he did not know for help in raising his son and getting him the food he needed to survive. During that prayer, he said, "God, if you'll save my boy, you can have him for any work you want him to do; you can even make him a preacher." It was the most sacrificial prayer he could think to pray. God heard my grandfather's prayer. My father was spared, and he grew up healthy.

As my father walked into his parents' bedroom that night following the revival meeting, he began to share how Jesus had changed his life. He said, "Dad, tonight my sins were forgiven, and I was saved, and I know God has called me to the ministry. I know I'm supposed to be a preacher. Is that OK with you?"

My grandfather replied, "Yes, it's OK. We've been expecting this to happen," and he told my father the story you just read. Six months later, both of my grandparents came to Christ. My grandfather served as a church leader for forty years, and my grandmother, who at this writing is 106 years old, has been involved for over seventy years in this same Assemblies of God church.

This is the heritage in which I was raised. My father attended Northwest University and planted churches in Spokane, Washington. He led me to Christ when I was five years old. That night is crystalized in my mind, even though I was very young.

As I grew up in a Pentecostal setting, with my father as my pastor, I can still remember seeing the evidence of the Holy Spirit in people's lives. People experienced some amazing healings and miracles, and I was introduced to the power of the Spirit. As a teen, I remember wrongly thinking that anyone who does not speak in tongues and is not filled with the Spirit is only a partial Christian. Part of my angst with this is that I had never spoken in tongues myself. It seemed like that was the decisive test of a real spiritual person. I know now that my theology was mistaken, but I was being trained and constantly modeled in that culture.

It was not that people filled with the Spirit shared their faith often with others, led people to Christ, or prayed with people openly outside of a church service. Those were not the standard marks of accepted spiritual maturity—speaking in tongues was. This was such a factor that tongues became the focus, rather than being filled with the Spirit, in order to be more effective at sharing the gospel.

In fact, it was regularly modeled for me by people I admired. They were significantly different on the street or downtown in our small community than they were in church. This difference in behavior became a norm that modeled for me repeatedly that "the Spirit-filled life is for church services only."

As I became older, I began to recognize some of the excesses and extremes in Pentecostalism. Loud wailing, interruptions in the service, and demonstrative behaviors set me back. Additionally, people who gave a message in tongues or a prophecy during the service, and then gossiped about other people in the church or performed deceptive business practices, further fueled my suspicions. I could see the power was real, but I could also see a counterfeit. I was determined to either seek the authentic experience or have nothing to do with being Pentecostal.

I headed to Bible camp the summer I was fifteen. During the evening service, the evangelist, Roy Brewer, gave the call for prayer to anyone who wanted to be baptized in the Holy Spirit. That was me, but I wanted the real deal. I did not want anyone praying with me or laying hands on me. I wanted to be alone with Jesus.

I am not saying it is wrong to pray with people or lay hands on them to receive the Holy Spirit. That is thoroughly biblical. I had seen some people praying with others, though, coaxing them to speak in tongues, and I wanted none of that. This experience was to be genuine, or I wanted nothing to do with it.

As I slipped to the end of a prayer bench, I began to pray, and nothing happened. I thought God was going to move my lips and muscles and form the new language coming out of my mouth. I honestly did not know how this worked. I was confused about the process and very concerned about it being authentic.

I prayed for about fifteen minutes with no results, and then a thought came into my mind on how to pray. With my simple understanding, I rebuked the Devil, so he would put no words in my mouth. Then I submitted to God, declaring that whatever he put in my mind, I would speak out in faith, believing he had put it there. I waited.

A moment later, a word came into my mind—at least I think it was a word. I did not understand it, and I felt very foolish speaking it aloud. I had made God a promise, though, so I did speak it… in a whisper. Then another word came and another and another, and soon I was whispering, then quietly speaking a language I had never learned. I was communicating to God in a heavenly language. The emotions of that moment overwhelmed me, as I was enveloped in the deep love of God's presence.

I have given a lot of reflection to this occurrence. Think for a moment about this experience and how language itself works. When we see something with our eyes, like a watch, for example, our brain recognizes the object and triggers the nerves in our mouth muscles to say, "watch." As we grow, we become very adept at forming words and recognizing objects.

Now think about this…

Can you tell me the name of something you do not know? Of course not. No one can, because we have no words for unknown objects.

When people speak in tongues, they are not just saying words they have never learned; they are speaking an entire language and communicating a message. This experience has a flow that is clear to anyone witnessing it, but I want to remind the reader again: speaking in tongues is not the focus.

The focus must be on the Holy Spirit's power to move the mission of Jesus forward. We will cover more on this topic later, but it is enough to say at this point that when someone speaks in tongues, it is clear to the speaker that he is talking to God. It is evident that this is a genuine, spiritual experience.

Being baptized in the Holy Spirit profoundly changed my life, adding a level of boldness for the gospel I had never known. My open witnessing at my high school shifted powerfully. My hunger for God's Word was obvious, and both my parents and those around me noticed the change. My sensitivity to the Holy Spirit increased.

It was a very special season in my life, and I was aware I was growing spiritually as never before.

Nevertheless, the church culture I experienced focused on expressions of the Holy Spirit being limited to weekly church services. Gradually, I felt myself being pulled back into the conformity that modeled that almost all Holy Spirit expressions, with very few exceptions, were to take place during a church service.

About two years later, during a time alone with God in my bedroom, I was called to ministry. The next obvious step for me was to go to college, so I attended Northwest University like my father and served eight years in youth ministry before taking my first church as lead pastor.

This church was located in Vader, in southwest Washington. The town had 350 people, and the church had about forty in regular attendance. We served here for the next six years, and it was a wonderful experience. I soon began to notice the tension building between these distinct philosophies of ministry, which we have outlined in the introduction.

As our church focused on being Pentecostal in our services, which I had had modeled so effectively for me, we experienced a deep sense of God's presence, and that became the focus of each service. The idea that our church was in this community to minister to it was a foreign thought. We all believed we were here to feel close to God. That was our purpose. As a result, we felt close to God, but hardly anyone new came to Christ in those early years.

This frustrated me greatly, and I began to search for another way. I then became aware of two primary fountainheads promoting what it meant to be a missional church, a completely new term for me. Those national influences were Rick Warren from Saddleback Church and Bill Hybels from Willow Creek Church, neither of which is Pentecostal.

Warren had a focus reaching the stereotypical resident named "Saddleback Sam," and he had designed an entire profile on this fictitious character. Hybels had coined a new phrase called "Seeker Sensitive", which meant a church should reexamine its procedures in the light of being an outreach-focused church. A seeker-sensitive church filters its language and service components so it is very relevant, and no one coming to a church service stumbles over anything, except the gospel of Jesus.

It is difficult to estimate the wonderful impact these two amazing leaders have had on our country and the world. Their insight into leadership and ways to help a church reach its community are amazing. I owe a debt to each of them for helping chart a way forward, and it is impossible to know how many people are following Jesus today because of them. Neither is Pentecostal, but they had something I needed. I then began leading our church to become missional in focus.

Interestingly enough, people began to come to Christ. As we toned down the "Spirit components" of the service and focused on teaching people to reach out, we saw our church begin to grow.

About this time, I moved to lead my second church in Lynden, Washington. It was a highly charismatic church, and as I led it towards becoming missional (outreach focused), I felt significant pushback. It became obvious that this church's culture was built on emotional experiences during the services, which they claimed to be Holy Spirit induced.

While I have no problem with emotions being affected by the move of the Spirit, I still sensed we needed to focus on reaching the lost in our community. It was almost like it was now an "either/or" proposition rather than a "both/and". Either we experienced the move of the Spirit, which satisfied the people in this church, or we toned down our charismatic services to reach out to lost people. This was the first time I began to face the great divide presented by these two philosophies. Did it really have to be "either/or"? Why was I being forced to choose? Why did my days at preacher school not deal with this? I was very frustrated.

My focus on reaching lost people and this church's cultural insistence on emotionally-driven services eventually reached a climax, when I was asked to leave as the pastor. It was painful, and I have given this story full treatment in my book, Turnaround Pastor. I am not blaming this church, as I have to take responsibility for my part in this, and certainly, this story has more to it. Nevertheless, it is important to understand this clash in ministry focus, and our lack of agreement on the purpose of the church played a significant part in my leaving.

This was a painful and difficult season. I sat out of pastoral ministry for the next two years, as I tried to understand what I had experienced, what my responsibility was, and how Jesus was going to use this in my life. Little did I know that my next assignment would take me to an even higher level of frustration and exploration.

In 1995, my wife Brenda and I came to lead North Seattle Christian Fellowship, which would later become Creekside Church. This church had been a two thousand-member flagship of the charismatic movement of the '70s and '80s. It was common for the three-hour service to be dominated by the voice gifts of the Spirit, with multiple tongues and prophecies. I attended this church as a student during my time at Northwest University and witnessed these services firsthand.

However, in 1995, this church was now 350 instead of two thousand members, and it was in steep decline. I, as well as the leadership, knew we needed to focus on outreach to have any kind of future. In my current understanding, this meant that being missional took first place over being Pentecostal. I still had not been able to reconcile the two different philosophies in my mind, so I felt like I had to do spiritual triage. Reaching lost people was more important than making the "already convinced" feel good during a service.

Those who were in the church believed church was strictly for them, services were for them, and especially my role as lead pastor was for them. The baptistery literally had dust in it, because it had not been used for so long. I was discussing this with the former lead pastor, Richard Vicknair, who had become my associate pastor. He said, "You must think people are far more open to the gospel than I've experienced." Yes, I did.

This Seattle church had been so extremely charismatic that the concept of the gifts of the Spirit being used in daily life was unheard of, as it is in many churches. In fact, the goal of the services had become, as in my first church, to "feel God's presence," and this Seattle church's culture modeled that the expression of the Holy Spirit's gifts was to make us feel good during our services. It was inconceivable that a service would happen without it being dominated by the voice gifts of prophecy, tongues, and interpretation.

While I knew that the Holy Spirit's gifts were real, something did not sit right in my heart. Somehow, feeling good about our worship experience, while most people in our neighborhoods were lost, seemed contrary to God's very nature. That "missional component" kept tugging at me. In fact, it went even further, because the focus of the service caused me to wonder if we were worshiping the gifts more than God himself.

I tread softly here, but it is entirely possible for us to worship our worship experience more than we worship God. We can worship worship more than God. It is entirely possible for us to worship the Word of God more than the God of the Bible, and it is entirely possible for us to worship the operation of the gifts of the Spirit more than the God who gave these gifts to us. It is, in a sense, idolatry of a most subtle nature, wherein we put our own experience ahead of the mission of Jesus.

However, the exact opposite is also true. It is entirely possible for us as church leaders and members to be so focused on reaching lost people that we ignore the power of the Holy Spirit given to us for just that purpose. We ignore his power because we are concerned that it could get out of hand and become extreme. Maybe people will go overboard, or some situations could become unruly.

Therefore, we restrain those we train and, instead, develop elaborate outreach strategies based on systems, ratios, and growth principles, all of which are good but will never replace the Holy Spirit's empowerment. In effect, we control rather than lead, and such leadership behavior is often rooted in fear. Nevertheless, an answer does exist.

CHAPTER TWO

HOLY SPIRIT EMPOWERED

MAYBE YOU ARE TEMPTED to look at this chapter title, say, "I already know this," and skim through the pages. May I ask you to set aside your assumptions and imagine for a few moments that you are a new believer again?

Reflect for a moment on the new life Christ has given you and the new world of faith into which you have been inducted. Something in your heart tells you this is bigger than you, and your new faith involves your friends and family, too. Your new relationship with Jesus will somehow impact those you know, and you are compelled to share this gospel and the way your life has changed.

That sentiment is exactly what every new believer feels when he or she first comes to Christ. This inner drive to share the gospel is either fed through obedience or starved by disobedience, but we all start here. Do you remember having that spiritual focus in your life?

An eighteen-year-old Japanese student came to live with my family some years ago. His name was Takeshi, and after living in our home a few months, he began to explore faith in Christ. As a part of this exploration, he chose to write a term paper for Seattle University, where he was attending, comparing the three monotheistic religions of Christianity, Islam, and Judaism. His primary observation was amazing (I was already surprised he chose to research this topic), and knowing I was a pastor, he asked to talk with me about his findings before turning in his paper.

We sat down to talk, and I said, "Takeshi, tell me what you've learned."

He replied, "There are many differences between all three, but one significant difference stands out to me. Christianity is the only religion that teaches a focus on the Holy Spirit, right?"

I was stunned by his primary observation, as I had never even thought about this before, but he was right. While Islam's Koran mentions the Holy Spirit four times, it does not teach a personal relationship with the Holy Spirit as Jesus taught his disciples. Judaism teaches more on the Holy Spirit, but again, it is more like a force in the lives of God followers than a personal empowerment of all followers of Judaism.

Takeshi's observation was correct. The emphasis of Christianity on the Holy Spirit is significantly more focused than that of either Islam or Judaism. This observation was from a young unbeliever exploring a personal faith in Christ.

Takeshi continued, "From my study, the Holy Spirit convicts believers of Jesus about sin, guides them into God's truth, and empowers them to give their faith away. Am I right?"

I said, "That is correct. There is more also, but everything you have said is accurate. Good job on your research paper."

After all, we were not doing a study on the Holy Spirit. He was just talking to me, a religious professional, to see if his facts were straight, and they were. My wife and I have hosted well over one hundred foreign students living with us over the last twenty years, and this is the only conversation like this I have ever had.

Little did I know my daughter Kelly had also been having "Jesus talks" with Takeshi, and about four months later at a youth conference, Takeshi accepted Christ. He called me at 10:00 pm after receiving Christ and said, "Don, I have just accepted Christ into my life. I know it is dark outside, but it is noon in my heart."

I will never forget that day. His new faith sparked a deep struggle with his parents, who rejected his faith and him for a short time, but he worked to heal those relationships. Then, three years later, this young man became my first son-in-law, and he and Kelly have given us three wonderful grandchildren. Today, he serves as an elder in the church we attend.

At one point after Takeshi came to Christ, he asked me, "Shouldn't we be out on the street, talking to people about Jesus?" He was showing concern for a lost and dying world, which was something he had not experienced before. We talked about how relational evangelism works and how to live as a good example. He then began to share Christ with friends and family.

As of this writing, Takeshi's entire family has been impacted by the gospel, although none are following Jesus yet. His mother is attending a Christian church in Tokyo to "learn English better," and his father has gone on two of our mission trips to Honduras.

The gospel of Jesus is a living, life-giving force inside us, designed to emerge and transform those around us.

WE ARE ON A MISSION

God sent Jesus to ransom the world and to save the world from sin, which is an enormous undertaking. Jesus was on a mission from God to bring salvation and transformation to the world. In order to do that, individual people need to be transformed by the saving power of faith in Christ.

> "The Son of Man did not come to be served, but to serve, and to give his life as a ransom for many." Matthew 20:28

As soon as we are transformed and redeemed, we are instantly called to be part of God's solution to help reach a lost and dying world. We are inducted immediately into the compassionate army of God. Jesus has called us to be a part of this mission of reaching lost men and women with the gospel.

In fact, in John 17, Jesus prays specifically for this. Just before he is arrested and crucified, he prays to his Father in front of the disciples that they will be sent out into the world. He prays that those of us who follow him will not be taken out of the world, but that we will be protected from Satan.

He prays we would be sanctified (set apart for a purpose) and then sent back into the world exactly like the Father sent him into the world. Jesus invites all of us who follow him to join him on his mission.

> "My prayer is not that you take them out of the world but that you protect them from the evil one. They are not of the world, even as I am not of it. Sanctify them by the truth; your word is truth. As you sent me into the world, I have sent them into the world." John 17:15-18

This is such an important message that Jesus repeats it again to his disciples immediately upon his resurrection, the very first time he sees them. This time, however, he adds something to his first message regarding the Holy Spirit. Jesus tells his disciples their assignment is still the same, but they are to receive additional help. They cannot do his mission alone. The disciples need to be empowered with the life of the Spirit to do God's will.

> "Again Jesus said, 'Peace be with you! As the Father has sent me, I am sending you.' And with that he breathed on them and said, 'Receive the Holy Spirit.'" John 20:21-22

With these words, Jesus reminds his disciples that he is sending them out in the same way the Father sent Jesus to the world. However, he ends with the words, "Receive the Holy Spirit" after breathing on them. Jesus has already told them he will be leaving, and then he will send the Holy Spirit. In fact, Jesus tells his disciples that it is for their good that he is leaving them and sending the Holy Spirit.

Why does Jesus breathe on the disciples? He has not done this exercise before. Does he stand in front of each one and breathe on them, or is it a collective group breath? John does not say, but it is memorable enough for him to record it in his gospel.

I do not know how Jesus breathed on his disciples, and for our purposes, that is not important. Nevertheless, here is a thought I believe is important, and it impacts every follower of Jesus—this is the second time God has breathed on man. The first time happened in the Garden, because God is the one who gives life to us all.

Genesis 2:7 reads, "Then the Lord God formed a man from the dust of the ground and breathed into his nostrils the breath of life." God gave humankind physical life by breathing into him the breath of life. God initiated our very life-breath. He breathed life into us, and without his breath, we would have no life at all.

I would like to suggest Jesus is showing the disciples the truth of the Holy Spirit's indwelling. By declaring his words again about the mission, sending his disciples out to speak about the Holy Spirit, and breathing on them, he is declaring that new life only comes by the Holy Spirit.

We are saved by the power of the Holy Spirit. Anyone who has come to faith in Christ has the Holy Spirit, even those who do not speak in tongues. Scripture tells us this in Romans 8:9, "You, however, are not in the realm of the flesh but are in the realm of the Spirit, if indeed the Spirit of God lives in you. And if anyone does not have the Spirit of Christ, they do not belong to Christ." Believers before the day of Pentecost then, had the Holy Spirit living in them.

But having the Holy Spirit live in us is not enough. We are empowered to share the gospel by the Holy Spirit. The solid truth is we will never live up to Christ's expectations to carry the gospel into all the world without the power of the Holy Spirit working through us.

LIFE IS BETTER WITH THE SPIRIT

It must have been difficult for the disciples to believe that it would be better for them with Jesus gone. Later, Jesus clearly explains why it is better for them. We understand now that Jesus, serving in a physical body, could only be in one place at a time, but the Holy Spirit (Advocate) fills believers' lives with his power all over the globe. However, the disciples are far from seeing that perspective. They are only grieving their personal loss.

> "But very truly I tell you, it is for your good that I am going away. Unless I go away, the Advocate will not come to you; but if I go, I will send him to you." John 16:7

Jesus tells his disciples the Holy Spirit will teach them and guide them, just as he has done. Then Jesus goes one step further and shares with his disciples about his very own close relationship with the Holy Spirit. He tells them that everything the Holy Spirit will show them will come directly from him.

> "He will glorify me because it is from me that he will receive what he will make known to you. All that belongs to the Father is mine. That is why I said the Spirit will receive from me what he will make known to you." John 16:14-15

Jesus is trying to comfort his disciples. They are afraid, because they are losing Jesus. He tells them he is going away, but the Holy Spirit will be their connection to him. Whatever the Holy Spirit gives them comes straight from Jesus.

These sections of Scripture include three key facts that stand out and are critical to our understanding. Each of these non-negotiables must be fully embraced to be part of God's mission to reach this world with the transforming message of the gospel. They are:

1. Jesus' mission from God was to come and save the world.

2. Jesus has called all of the redeemed to join him on this mission.

3. We must be empowered by the Holy Spirit to do this mission.

To accomplish this mission of reaching lost people, Jesus asks his disciples to wait to be empowered by the Holy Spirit. After his resurrection and just a short time before he is taken up into heaven, he tells them not to leave Jerusalem because the gift of the Holy Spirit is coming. This is a gift from Jesus to them, and because they love and trust Jesus, their hearts are open to receive his gift.

> "Do not leave Jerusalem, but wait for the gift my Father promised, which you have heard me speak about. For John baptized with water, but in a few days you will be baptized with the Holy Spirit." Acts 1:4-5

Jesus confirms what John the Baptist spoke about in the opening chapters of the New Testament. John the Baptist was not just to prepare the way for the Jesus the Messiah to bring the gospel of salvation. John was also preparing the way for those who followed Jesus to personally receive the Holy Spirit from Jesus.

> "I baptize you with water for repentance. But after me comes one who is more powerful than I, whose sandals I am not worthy to carry. He will baptize you with the Holy Spirit and fire." Matthew 3:11

John the Baptist defines two baptisms in this verse—a "baptism of repentance" and a "baptism with the Holy Spirit." John was called to baptize people publically in water for repentance, but Jesus is the one who baptizes us in the Holy Spirit. John also makes it clear that Jesus is much more powerful than he is.

In the opening verses of the gospel of John, John the Baptist repeats this same fact again as he testifies to what he saw during Jesus' baptism. Jesus is the one who baptizes us in the Holy Spirit. This baptism of the Spirit is Jesus' personal gift to any believer who follows Jesus.

> "And I myself did not know him, but the one who sent me to baptize with water told me, 'The man on whom you see the Spirit come down and remain is the one who will baptize with the Holy Spirit.'" John 1:33

This is the first time the word baptize is used in this gospel. Evangelicals debate as to whether or not the terms born of the Spirit and baptized in the Holy Spirit have the same meaning. Let me be clear—I do not believe they have the same meaning. Jesus taught his disciples the two levels of relationship they would have with the Holy Spirit.

In Jesus' famous conversation with Nicodemus, the teacher of Israel, he introduces the concept of being "born of the Spirit." Jesus compares two kinds of births—a birth of the flesh, as when a new baby is born into the world, and a spiritual birth given by the Holy Spirit.

> "Jesus answered, 'Very truly I tell you, no one can enter the kingdom of God unless they are born of water and the Spirit. Flesh gives birth to flesh, but the Spirit gives birth to spirit. You should not be surprised at my saying, "You must be born again." The wind blows wherever it pleases. You hear its sound, but you cannot tell where it

24

comes from or where it is going. So it is with everyone born of the Spirit.'" John 3:5-8

This is confounding to the scholar Nicodemus, who is familiar with and has taught on the Holy Spirit. He knows of the Holy Spirit from his study of the Scriptures and the way the Spirit came upon the prophets and leaders throughout Israel's history. However, Nicodemus is unaware of the Spirit giving a new birth to people. This is a strange and new concept to him. Jesus gently scolds Nicodemus in John 3:10 by saying, "You are Israel's teacher, and you don't understand these things?"

In this conversation, Jesus is teaching all of us that our relationship with the Holy Spirit begins when we receive "new birth," and the Holy Spirit gives us this life. Salvation happens with repentance, and we are "born of the Spirit." This is our first and primary relationship with the Holy Spirit, but it does not end there, as Jesus taught his disciples.

In the last week of Jesus' life, before going to the cross, he spends time teaching his disciples about the Holy Spirit, and in one conversation, he defines two levels of our relationship with the Holy Spirit.

> "If you love me, keep my commands. And I will ask the Father, and he will give you another Advocate to help you and be with you forever—the Spirit of truth. The world cannot accept him, because it neither sees him nor knows him. But you know him, for he lives with you and will be in you." John 14:15-17

In this Scripture, Jesus teaches us several important truths. He begins with telling us how he knows if we love him. Jesus' standard of love is obedience. Period. To Jesus, genuine love equals obedience. It is critical to understand this, because obedience opens the door to everything in the life of the Spirit. Knowledge, experience, education, and status are all secondary. This may seem simplistic, but it is not. Obedience defines who is in charge of our lives.

Then Jesus tells his disciples that he will ask the Father to send "another advocate." In saying this, Jesus is reminding his disciples that he is their Advocate (their Comforter and one who stands with them), and he is sending them another just like him. The language Jesus uses here is significant, illustrated by the Greek words being used.

The Greek language uses two words for the word *another* - "allos", meaning "another of the same kind," and "heteros", meaning "another of a different kind." Jesus uses the word "allos" here. He is saying, "I know you are sad because I'm leaving, but take heart. I am sending you another Advocate who is just like me in nature and essence. The Holy Spirit will be with you as I am with you."

It is important that we draw the connection between Jesus and the Holy Spirit, because we live in a compartmentalized world. We like to categorize ideas or concepts in order to understand them, and we may have done that with our understanding of the Godhead. While Jesus clearly teaches us the doctrine of the Trinity, and I fully subscribe to this doctrine, Jesus more often draws our attention to the connection between the Holy Spirit and himself. To have a relationship with Jesus is to have a relationship with the Holy Spirit.

The only way we will ever be able to live up to Jesus' expectations and move the mission of Jesus forward is through the power of the Holy Spirit. We have no other option.

CHAPTER THREE
I.P.E.

WE KNOW WE RECEIVE the Holy Spirit in our lives when we come to faith in Jesus, but Scripture speaks of an empowering from the Holy Spirit that comes into believers after they have believed. Having the power of the Holy Spirit in your life to do the mission of Jesus is critical, but how do you know when this has happened? In this chapter, we enter into a discussion about such evidence.

Let me declare from the outset that I am not a crusader on this question, and my findings will not remove all doubt. However, I needed to settle this question for myself, so I am inviting you to join me on a journey of discovery.

The primary evidence for tongues as the initial physical evidence is laid out in Scripture in the book of Acts, which is where we will focus. It seems prudent to discuss how we are individually empowered by the Spirit, or "filled with the Spirit," before we discuss how local churches are empowered, which is why we have written this chapter.

If you were raised in a Pentecostal church or attended a Pentecostal university, then you know the letters at the beginning of this chapter stand for Initial Physical Evidence (I.P.E.) as it relates to the baptism in the Holy Spirit. People in some circles debate as to what the evidence of this experience is, which is why we are addressing it here.

The subject of evidence is an interesting topic. While at my first church, I served as a jury foreman in a trial in which criminal charges were filed. This fascinating experience forced me to understand evidence on a deeper level than ever before.

If you have ever served on a jury and discussed evidence from a legal point of view, you know the three basic kinds of evidence:

Preponderance of evidence. This has to do with probable truth or accuracy of the evidence, as well as the amount of evidence. This evidence is used often in civil cases.

Circumstantial evidence. This evidence relies on an inference of circumstances to connect it to a logical conclusion.

Evidence beyond reasonable doubt. This is the primary standard of evidence required for a criminal conviction in most legal systems. The prosecutor bears the burden of proof and is required to prove his case.

As we walk through the evidence below, we will look briefly at the history of the term "initial physical evidence" and the first two types of evidence in the Scriptures in the book of Acts. While we are not trying a legal case, the word "evidence" has nevertheless become part of the discussion. We will look at this topic from that direction, not as attorneys, but as biblical students.

INITIAL PHYSICAL EVIDENCE: OUR HISTORY

What constitutes evidence for being baptized in the Holy Spirit from a biblical perspective continues to be a lively discussion among Pentecostals, but in our own fellowship of the Assemblies of God, it is a settled question.

How did we get to this place, and why do we believe speaking in tongues is the initial physical evidence of being baptized in the Holy Spirit? Perhaps some history is needed for a more complete understanding.

The Roots of "Initial Physical Evidence"

In Gordon Robertson's article entitled "The Roots of Azusa: Pentecost in Topeka," he states the following:

"In October 1900 in Topeka, Kansas, a small band of believers led by Charles Parham started Bethel Bible School. The school "invited all ministers and Christians who were willing to forsake all, sell what they had, give it away, and enter the school for study and prayer, where all of us together might trust God for food, fuel, rent and clothing." No one paid tuition or board and they all wanted to be equipped to go to the ends of the earth to preach the gospel of the Kingdom as a witness to every nation. The only textbook was the Bible. Their concerted purpose was to learn the Bible not just in their heads but to have each thing in the Scriptures wrought out in their hearts.

"As they searched the scriptures, they came up with one great problem—what about the second chapter of Acts? In December 1900, Parham sent his students at work to diligently search the scriptures for the Biblical evidence of the baptism in the Holy Spirit. They all came back with the same answer—when the baptism in the Holy Spirit came to the early disciples, the indisputable proof on each occasion was that they spoke with other tongues."

Historically, the language of the initial physical evidence came from here and became a significant part of the foundation of Pentecostal theology.

Dr. Donald Detrick, Associate Network Leader of the Northwest Ministry Network and history professor at Northwest University, cites:

"Regarding the Initial Evidence and Parham posing the question to his students, it is documented in several sources. I recall Dr. Gary McGee, author of "People of the Spirit," the definitive Assembly of God history, tell the story many times as one of my professors at seminary.

"Although Parham himself was discredited later in life in many ways, the Assemblies of God continues to cite his question about "Bible evidence" which we have morphed into "initial physical evidence." That was a question that the people of God were asking as we ushered in the 20th century.

"In addition, we hold up William Seymour for his role in Azusa Street, which we should rightly do. However, we disregard the fact that he never became a part of the Assemblies of God and by the time the Assemblies of God was formed in 1914, the Azusa revival had been over for nearly 5 years, and he had abandoned the initial evidence doctrine."

Reading about two primary voices of the past, Parham and Seymour, and knowing that Pentecostals stand on this "initial evidence" as a doctrinal keystone, let us look at the biblical evidence for ourselves.

INITIAL PHYSICAL EVIDENCE FROM ACTS

Five key places in the book of Acts offer proof that speaking in tongues is the initial evidence of the baptism in the Holy Spirit. Consider first the words "initial" and "physical".

Clearly, the Scripture teaches many evidences of the Holy Spirit using and empowering a believer. We do not dispute that. We are simply saying from the biblical proof, speaking in tongues is the first evidence, hence the word "initial". Since speaking in tongues is heard, this makes it "physical" evidence.

Initial evidence does not mean the only evidence, just the first physical evidence. As we look through these five specific Scriptures, consider them as evidence, and review them for yourself.

#1: The Outpouring of the Holy Spirit, Acts 2:1-4

Acts 2:1-4 is the first recorded incident of believers being baptized in the Holy Spirit.

> "When the day of Pentecost came, they were all together in one place. Suddenly a sound like the blowing of a violent wind came from heaven and filled the whole house

where they were sitting. They saw what seemed to be tongues of fire that separated and came to rest on each of them. All of them were filled with the Holy Spirit and began to speak in other tongues as the Spirit enabled them."

This Scripture in Acts 2 is the fulfillment of Jesus' words which he gives to his disciples in Acts 1, just before he is taken up into heaven.

"On one occasion, while he was eating with them, he gave them this command: "Do not leave Jerusalem, but wait for the gift my Father promised, which you have heard me speak about. For John baptized with water, but in a few days you will be baptized with the Holy Spirit." Acts 1:4-5

The focus in Acts 2:4 shows the distinct link between speaking in tongues and being baptized in the Holy Spirit. All of those in the upper room are filled with the Holy Spirit, and the first physical act following this Holy Spirit filling is for each of them to speak in other tongues as the Spirit enables them.

#2: The Apostles and Simon in Samaria, Acts 8:9-24

The second mention of the baptism in the Holy Spirit is in Acts 8:14-24. It is the story of Peter and John in Samaria, where they meet Simon, who practices sorcery.

"Now for some time a man named Simon had practiced sorcery in the city and amazed all the people of Samaria. He boasted that he was someone great, and all the people, both high and low, gave him their attention and exclaimed,

'This man is rightly called the Great Power of God.' They followed him because he had amazed them for a long time with his sorcery. But when they believed Philip as he proclaimed the good news of the kingdom of God and the name of Jesus Christ, they were baptized, both men and women. Simon himself believed and was baptized. And he followed Philip everywhere, astonished by the great signs and miracles he saw." Acts 8:9-13

In this passage of Scripture, Philip is doing the work of an evangelist and bringing people to faith in Christ. God is confirming this work with signs and miracles, to the point that the noted sorcerer Simon, whom many people follow, now puts his faith in Christ.

Because of this revival in Samaria, many people, including Simon, are baptized. Obviously, this baptism is the baptism in water into the name of Jesus (verse 16 below) and not the baptism of the Holy Spirit; otherwise, the following verses would not be necessary.

"When the apostles in Jerusalem heard that Samaria had accepted the word of God, they sent Peter and John to Samaria. When they arrived, they prayed for the new believers there that they might receive the Holy Spirit, because the Holy Spirit had not yet come on any of them; they had simply been baptized in the name of the Lord Jesus. Then Peter and John placed their hands on them, and they received the Holy Spirit." Acts 8:14-17

The apostles in Jerusalem now send Peter and John to investigate how the gospel is affecting this region of Samaria. Peter and John first pray for these new believers to receive the Holy Spirit, which tells us two critical observations.

First, it tells us the apostles believe it is critical for new believers to be baptized in the Holy Spirit. Paul in Ephesus (19:2), along with

Peter and John, discover that the new believers in Samaria (8:16) had not been baptized in the Holy Spirit. They each saw this experience as both an opportunity and an expectation.

In their opinion, it is not enough to simply believe and be baptized in water in Jesus' name. Let us remember these men walked with Jesus, the One who told them to wait and be baptized in the Holy Spirit.

If Jesus believes it is important to be baptized in the Holy Spirit, and the apostles believe it is important for followers of Jesus to be baptized in the Holy Spirit, we need to believe and teach this as well.

Second, this Scripture tells us that these apostles know it is possible to believe and not be baptized in the Holy Spirit. They teach putting one's faith in Christ and being baptized in the Holy Spirit are two different and distinct faith steps for believers to take.

Now the rest of this story gives us further evidence regarding being baptized in the Holy Spirit.

> "When Simon saw that the Spirit was given at the laying on of the apostles' hands, he offered them money and said, "Give me also this ability so that everyone on whom I lay my hands may receive the Holy Spirit.

> "Peter answered: 'May your money perish with you, because you thought you could buy the gift of God with money! You have no part or share in this ministry, because your heart is not right before God. Repent of this wickedness and pray to the Lord in the hope that he may forgive you for having such a thought in your heart. For I see that you are full of bitterness and captive to sin.'

> "Then Simon answered, 'Pray to the Lord for me so that nothing you have said may happen to me.' Acts 8:18-24

While this Scripture never says the Samaritan believers spoke in tongues, and speaking in tongues is never mentioned in this story, we do know something happened. Simon saw something. The Samaritan believers had a way of knowing who was and who was not baptized in the Holy Spirit.

When Peter and John pray for the new believers, and they are baptized in the Holy Spirit, Simon witnesses some evidence of this experience. The apostles pray, the believers receive, and Simon witnesses something physical; otherwise, the Scripture would not have said in verse 18, "When Simon saw the Spirit was given …"

Something physical happens in this moment for Simon to "see." Again, while the Scriptures do not say the new believers who were baptized in the Holy Spirit spoke in tongues, Acts contains evidence that this is exactly what happened. Remember, Peter and John are both in the upper room in Acts 2, and they know what being baptized in the Holy Spirit looks and sounds like.

Since we are to examine all Scripture, remember we are looking at five examples of Holy Spirit baptism from the book of Acts. Peter will later tell us in Acts 10:44-48 exactly how he knows when someone is baptized in the Holy Spirit. It is reasonable to assume that Peter uses the same decisive test in Acts 8 that he uses in Acts 10, which is speaking in tongues.

#3: Paul is Filled with the Holy Spirit, Acts 9:1-19

The third incident of someone being filled with the Holy Spirit in Acts is the story of the apostle Paul, who is called Saul in this story, as he has not changed his name yet. He was a first-century terrorist of such, looking to do God a service by arresting, imprisoning, and even executing Jesus' disciples. He becomes a major player in the New Testament, and God uses him to write over half of the New Testament.

"Meanwhile, Saul was still breathing out murderous threats against the Lord's disciples. He went to the high priest and asked him for letters to the synagogues in Damascus, so that if he found any there who belonged to the Way, whether men or women, he might take them as prisoners to Jerusalem. As he neared Damascus on his journey, suddenly a light from heaven flashed around him. He fell to the ground and heard a voice say to him, 'Saul, Saul, why do you persecute me?

"'Who are you, Lord?' Saul asked.

"'I am Jesus, whom you are persecuting,' he replied. 'Now get up and go into the city, and you will be told what you must do.'

"The men traveling with Saul stood there speechless; they heard the sound but did not see anyone. Saul got up from the ground, but when he opened his eyes he could see nothing. So they led him by the hand into Damascus. For three days he was blind, and did not eat or drink anything.

"In Damascus there was a disciple named Ananias. The Lord called to him in a vision, 'Ananias!'

"'Yes, Lord,' he answered.

"The Lord told him, 'Go to the house of Judas on Straight Street and ask for a man from Tarsus named Saul, for he is praying. In a vision he has seen a man named Ananias come and place his hands on him to restore his sight.'

"'Lord,' Ananias answered, 'I have heard many reports about this man and all the harm he has done to your holy people in Jerusalem. And he has come here with authority from the chief priests to arrest all who call on your name.'

"But the Lord said to Ananias, 'Go! This man is my chosen instrument to proclaim my name to the Gentiles and their kings and to the people of Israel. I will show him how much he must suffer for my name.'

"Then Ananias went to the house and entered it. Placing his hands on Saul, he said, 'Brother Saul, the Lord—Jesus, who appeared to you on the road as you were coming here—has sent me so that you may see again and be filled with the Holy Spirit.' Immediately, something like scales fell from Saul's eyes, and he could see again. He got up and was baptized, and after taking some food, he regained his strength." Acts 9:1-19

This is the account of Paul being saved and filled with the Holy Spirit. Verse 5 tells us how Paul meets Jesus, and verse 17 tells us Paul is filled with the Holy Spirit.

This story, as with the believers in Samaria, makes no mention of speaking in tongues. However, we know that Paul did speak in tongues, because he tells us this is the case. In 1 Corinthians 14:18 he says, "I thank God that I speak in tongues more than all of you."

Therefore, the question arises, "When did Paul first speak in tongues?" We do not know the answer to that question, but we know he did. The examples set forth in Acts chapters 2, 10, and 19 illustrate that speaking in tongues is part of being baptized in the Holy Spirit, also referred to as being "filled with the Holy Spirit."

Ananias lays hands on Paul for both his healing and for the filling of the Holy Spirit. Immediately after this act, Paul is filled with the Holy Spirit, his eyes are healed, and he is baptized in water, presumably into the name of Jesus. The terms, "baptized in the Holy Spirit" and "filled with the Holy Spirit", appear to be synonymous in Acts.

Although we cannot prove that Paul begins to speak in tongues at this point in his life, it seems plausible to think so.

Since the writer of Acts is Dr. Luke, and he wrote all the accounts of the baptism in the Holy Spirit in the book of Acts, he would have first-hand knowledge of how to know when another person is filled with the Holy Spirit. Luke identifies Paul as being filled with the Spirit; apparently, Paul qualifies.

#4: Peter at the House of Cornelius in Caesarea, Acts 10:44-48

The fourth occasion in the book of Acts of someone being baptized in the Holy Spirit is in Caesarea on a military base. I would recommend a fresh reading of the entire chapter of Acts 10. It is clear God wants to shift the early church culture in this story.

God challenges Cornelius, a God-fearing and generous Roman centurion, with a vision in which he communicates with an angel who gives orders for his next spiritual step—to send to Joppa for a man named Peter.

The next day, Peter falls into a trance, and God speaks to him as well about taking his next spiritual step. God illustrates what Peter had called "unclean" (meaning the Gentiles), was no longer to be called "unclean." The message becomes clearer to Peter when someone knocks at the door, and he is invited to come into a Gentile home. This is a first for him, and because God has prepared his heart, he goes.

Peter goes to Cornelius' house, and they each greet one another and tell their stories. Peter then begins to preach to the house full of people about the gospel of Jesus, but he is promptly interrupted.

Several interesting points stand out in this story, and I am fascinated by the progression and work of the Holy Spirit in this chapter.

First of all, Peter is a Jew, and he has always held to the law. It was a monumental personal shift for him to consider breaking the law. At this point in history, the Jesus-following Jews have essentially added faith in Christ to their Jewish traditions. It will be another ten years, approximately, that this debate will continue. It is not until the Council of Jerusalem, around A.D. 50, that the topic of Gentiles coming to Christ is fully settled in the church. Peter is a doctrinal trendsetter with this visit to Cornelius' home.

The second issue that stands out is that it does not seem to make much difference to the apostles whether new believers are baptized in water after being baptized in the Spirit, or the other way around. In the five accounts in Acts, we see it both ways.

Finally, the most critical piece of evidence for our topic is listed in verses 44-48 in which Peter identifies his litmus test of when someone is baptized in the Holy Spirit.

> "While Peter was still speaking these words, the Holy Spirit came on all who heard the message. The circumcised believers who had come with Peter were astonished that the gift of the Holy Spirit had been poured out even on Gentiles. For they heard them speaking in tongues and praising God.

> "Then Peter said, 'Surely no one can stand in the way of their being baptized with water. They have received the Holy Spirit just as we have.' So he ordered that they be baptized in the name of Jesus Christ. Then they asked Peter to stay with them for a few days." Acts 10:44-48

As is evident, in Peter's opinion, the key indicator that someone has been baptized in the Holy Spirit is that they have spoken in tongues. As a result of hearing these new believers speak in tongues, he declares, "no one can stand in the way of their being baptized with water," which was the public declaration of their faith in Christ.

Peter's words, "They have received the Holy Spirit just as we have," indicate that all the apostles received the Holy Spirit this way as well, since "we" refers to the apostles. Peter's viewpoint on this subject is certain; he makes it abundantly clear with his words.

#5: Paul and the Believers at Ephesus, Acts 19:1-7

The final story from Acts that talks about the baptism in the Holy Spirit is with Paul's missionary journey to Ephesus. Paul has now been established as a church leader with a calling and passion for reaching the Gentiles. The question about first becoming a Jew before following Jesus has been settled, and even some Pharisees (Acts 15:5) are now following Jesus.

Paul continues his missionary focus towards the Gentiles and reaches the city of Ephesus, where he finds some disciples. The first question he asks them is significant to our study.

> "While Apollos was at Corinth, Paul took the road through the interior and arrived at Ephesus. There he found some disciples and asked them, 'Did you receive the Holy Spirit when you believed?'

> "They answered, 'No, we have not even heard that there is a Holy Spirit.'

> "So Paul asked, 'Then what baptism did you receive?'

> "'John's baptism,' they replied.

> "Paul said, 'John's baptism was a baptism of repentance.

He told the people to believe in the one coming after him, that is, in Jesus.' On hearing this, they were baptized in the name of the Lord Jesus. When Paul placed his hands on them, the Holy Spirit came on them, and they spoke in tongues and prophesied. There were about twelve men in all." Acts 19:1-7

Paul's question, "Did you receive the Holy Spirit when you believed?" tells us something significant. Paul believes that it is possible to believe and not receive the Holy Spirit, in terms of being baptized in the Holy Spirit. This is a similar experience in Acts 8:15-17 when Peter and John in Samaria also believe it is possible to believe and follow Jesus and not "receive" the Holy Spirit. They are all speaking of a second and distinct work of grace called "the baptism in the Holy Spirit".

When I asked Dr. Waldemar Kowalski, Professor of Bible and Theology at Northwest University and member of the Theology Commission for the Assemblies of God, to review my observations on the passage, he had an interesting response.

He stated, "The question from verse two, 'Did you receive the Holy Spirit when you believed?' makes no sense theologically. The answer must be "yes", because of the indwelling of the Holy Spirit in the lives of all believers. Logically, though, the answer was "no", because they were not yet aware there was a Holy Spirit. In fact, most English Bibles will have a note to the word "when" indicating that in Greek this word also means "after." Many translators reject translations using the word "after", as it supports a Pentecostal understanding of subsequence, that is the Baptism of/in/by the Holy Spirit is subsequent to salvation. I would note that the word "after" is not only a possible translation, but in fact the only one that makes sense here."

When Paul then asks under what baptism these Ephesian believers are baptized, they say, "John's baptism." Paul explains that this is a baptism of repentance, and then he "re-baptizes" them into the name of Jesus. This is also a significant act.

As a pastor in the very Catholic city of Seattle, I saw many people come to Christ, then ask if they should be baptized again, since their parents baptized them as an infant. They asked if any Scripture in the Bible refers to people being re-baptized, and these verses became very helpful in those conversations.

Finally, Paul baptizes them in water and then lays hands on them. They are baptized in the Holy Spirit, then speak in tongues and prophesy. Speaking in tongues is again included in the evidence of Luke's narrative as the key indicator that these Ephesian believers have had the Holy Spirit descend on them.

WHY TONGUES?

Why would God choose tongues as an initial indicator that someone had been baptized in the Holy Spirit? The simple answer is I do not know, and neither do you. God is sovereign, and he can do whatever he wants. Nevertheless, I would like to suggest a thought here from Jesus' little brother, James.

> "Likewise, the tongue is a small part of the body, but it makes great boasts. Consider what a great forest is set on fire by a small spark. The tongue also is a fire, a world of evil among the parts of the body. It corrupts the whole body, sets the whole course of one's life on fire, and is itself set on fire by hell.

> "All kinds of animals, birds, reptiles, and sea creatures are being tamed and have been tamed by mankind, but no human being can tame the tongue. It is a restless evil, full of deadly poison." James 3:5-8

If the tongue is the unruliest part of the body, and Scripture says that no man can tame the tongue, then perhaps God has chosen to tame it himself. What if God said, "I'm going to take the member of the body that is the most unholy and use it for a holy purpose"?

If God can use our worst member for his best purposes, and if we yield our tongue to God for his glory, instead of our own, then Christ's character is being built into us every time we speak in tongues.

This does not mean after we are baptized in the Holy Spirit we will never hurt anyone with words or say evil things. We still have that choice. It does mean we can allow God to use our tongues for a holy purpose that will produce spiritual strength in a unique and powerful way.

After all, is that not the way of our Father, to take our worst and use it for his best, to take our evil and use it for his good? That is exactly what it means for our God to be a Redeemer.

A second consideration for what happened at Pentecost with the outpouring of the Holy Spirit and the manifestation of tongues, is very similar to the Old Testament story of the Tower of Babel in Genesis 11. In this story it is an act of judgement, but in Acts it is God's grace and empowering. My friend and colleague, Dr. Dave Cole, in his book, *Re-focus: Creating an Outward-Focused Church Culture* writes:

"God used situations like the Tower of Babel (Gen. 11) to disperse colonized people and send them around the world. In both the Babel and the Upper Room account found in Acts chapter two. He used the human tongue as a means to disperse the people. The first encounter at Babel came as God's judgment on humanity's pride. Rather than following His command to multiply and fill the earth, they chose to inhabit one city and build one culture. As a result of their rebellion, all of the residents received different languages from God. This experience served to form new groups of people, with different languages and cultures, who set out to populate the world.

"The second experience came to the Jewish believers in Acts

chapter two, as they were obeying Jesus' command to wait for the empowerment of the Holy Spirit. God chose to use tongues again. However, this time the new tongues received in the Upper Room, were not forced or given out of judgment. They were given by the grace of God to the Jewish believers as a sign of the empowerment of the Holy Spirit. The empowerment enabled them to disperse from Jerusalem and begin sharing the good news through the power of the Holy Spirit, to all people groups inhabiting the world."

Similarly, our home church pastor, Jason Deuman, in a conversation with me on this topic said, "The outpouring of the Holy Spirit at Pentecost, with the gift of tongues, shows how God reverses the curse of Babel. Instead of scattering the nations through languages, the praises of God are being proclaimed in different languages. The single event of Pentecost ties the mission of the gospel to reach all nations to the empowerment of the Spirit."

Again, our God shows himself to be a Redeemer. What was once used to scatter is now used to gather. What was once a curse is now a blessing.

CHAPTER FOUR
IT'S A LONG STORY

THE CHURCH FROM THE BOOK OF ACTS TO THE TWENTIETH CENTURY

AS AN HISTORIAN, I (Josh) am always excited to dig into the past and learn new stories. Just like a journalist looking forward to interviewing interesting new subjects, I am thrilled when I am introduced to a new part of the past. I will be honest—like most of us, what tends to interest me the most are stories connected to my own life and experience. In this chapter, I am going to make the case that despite often being overlooked by many Pentecostals, the long history of the entire church holds importance to our faith and to us.

Learning about our ancestors, digging into our histories, and exploring our own stories can be deeply inspiring. It is this level—the level of story—that is foundationally important. You see, each of us individually and (at times) corporately have stories we live and tell that help show us who we are. My story? I am a Pentecostal Christian. A college professor. A minister. A husband. An historian. A son and, Lord willing, perhaps one day a father. These are pieces of my personal narrative.

As you read this book, you are likely coming to it with stories that are rather different from mine. Yet, at the same time, I suspect that your continued interest in reading a book like this indicates that we share other life narratives. Most notable among these are probably connections to ministry and to the work of the Holy Spirit.

WHAT'S OUR STORY?

When I meet new people for the first time, I sometimes like to catch them off guard with a slightly odd question. After being introduced and learning their name, I ask the following: "What's your story?" Sure, it throws people off balance at first… but then that is just part of the fun. What and how they answer can potentially be very interesting. Consider, then, what Don and I have written in this book as our attempt to look at Pentecostals and to answer that same question: "What's our story?"

My part in answering this question is, at least in part, historical. I believe that knowing where we have been—and more importantly, what God has been doing in the lives of Christians over time—is helpful for understanding our place as heirs to that same story. After all, the Holy Spirit's work in and through Christian believers is not exhausted in the pages of the New Testament. It continues from that time until today.

That, my friends, is our story.

Many people know the story of the contemporary Pentecostal Movement of our time and its beginnings in the early twentieth century. Azusa Street, the Pentecostal missions movement, and the exploding numbers of those around the world today who testify to God's transforming Spirit are all part of this. It is an inspiring tale, and one that I look forward to discussing. Nevertheless, to start, I would like to do something different.

"Mind the gap." If you have ever traveled to London, you have probably heard this statement. Their subway system (called the "Tube") is an efficient and easy way to get around the city. It is a safe way to travel, but it needs a little instruction for newcomers. One of these instructions is to "mind the gap." In other words, travelers need to watch out for the space between the train and the platform as they step from one to the other. Being stuck in between would be problematic at best and potentially deadly at worst. Thankfully, it can be resolved by simply paying attention to what can so easily be overlooked.

In the next few pages, I would like to look at a part of our story that is not always recognized as such. I want us, in other words, to "mind the gap" in our collective memory. For as much as Spirit-filled believers love reflecting on God's powerful work in the first-century church and the revival of the twentieth century, the rest of history can often be ignored. I think that is a mistake. To not consider what God was up to in those "in-between" times is more than just an oversight. It represents a major missing piece to our story of faith.

Even though no "Pentecostal" denominations existed from the second through the nineteenth centuries, God's Spirit was still at work blessing, empowering, and equipping Christ followers. Though unfamiliar and even a little strange at times, what was taking place was still a part of the same Pentecostal story we share.

AFTER ACTS: THE SPIRIT IN THE FIRST CENTURIES OF THE CHURCH

Following the passions of a first-century church alive in the fire of the Spirit, the progression of time and realities of growth ensued. Missionary beginnings and charismatic giftings were in the New Testament, but the work of organizing and administering the developing church fell to subsequent eras. As elsewhere, a desire for structure and order could come at the expense of more unpredictable and enthusiastic actions. While it is unclear exactly what led to a decline from an Acts- or Corinthian-style Christianity, it is likely a progression towards organization and order had at least something to do with it.

Whatever the reason, it seems that fewer instances of believers embracing the Spirit in the Pentecostal sense are recorded after the biblical era. However—and this is important—this is not to say that God's miraculous work of the Spirit was absent. Take, for instance, the instructions of an early Christian manual called the *Didache*, dating from around the second century. In the midst of instructions about baptism and the life of faith is a guide for Christians who find themselves face to face with a traveling prophet. Among other directives, it says, "While a prophet is making ecstatic utterances, you must not test or examine him," before going on to say, "not everybody making ecstatic utterances is a prophet, but only if he behaves like the Lord. It is by their conduct that the false prophet and the [true] prophet can be distinguished."[1] It is common-sense advice, it seems, for a charismatic congregation.

Interesting, is it not? As an historian, I am fascinated by such a unique insight into the life of the early church. As a Pentecostal, I am even more excited to know that the Holy Spirit was miraculously working in certain figures during this period. Indeed, the fact that the author or authors of the *Didache* felt compelled to leave written instructions on what should be done means that this must have been more than just a one-time occurrence. Prophets, prophecy, you name it—in at least some parts of the church, this was still happening after the book of Acts concluded.

A group in these early centuries—the Montanists—fully exhibited some of the same Spirit-focused passions of modern Pentecostals. Often derided as heretics (and indeed they may have gone too far), this later second-century group believed that the Spirit could speak through human individuals and that deep spiritual experiences had a place in one's faith. They also, somewhat unusual for their time, had women in significant leadership roles in their movement.

The miraculous stories of some of the early martyrs also point to a Christianity that was quite open to the supernatural work of God. I am reminded here of Polycarp, a second-century believer who, late in life, was martyred under the Romans. In existing accounts, he is presented as a man of inspiring faith who bore witness to his Savior even to the end. Furthermore, upon his death by burning, the story indicates "we perceived such a sweet-smelling savour, as though from the breath of incense, or some other precious perfume."[2] This is not at all what you would expect from human flesh being burned on a pyre. At once amazing and not a little bizarre, it is testimony to a mindset open to the possibilities of God's miraculous power.

Another fascinating story of witness-unto-death (indeed, the word martyr actually means "witness" in the original Greek!) is the tale of Perpetua and Felicity. These two women—one a nursing mother and the other a pregnant slave—were arrested for their Christian faith and faced death in the arena. Perpetua had a fascinating spiritual vision before facing her fate. In that vision, she saw herself as a kind of gladiator fighting in the ring against an evil opponent. The implications for what was about to take place are obvious.

While legitimate questions can be asked about each of these stories and the many others that appear through early and medieval Christianity, I come to these stories as someone who shares at least a part of their openness to God's miraculous work. After all, how differently might I appreciate the story if a missionary told it to me last Sunday in service?

As Pentecostals, we firmly believe that God's Spirit moves in miraculous ways. Since we know he does so today, then we should also be open to these accounts from the past. If such accounts carry with them even seeds of truth, they reveal much more about our shared story than we might have previously thought. Furthermore, these stories were told and retold. They were a part of the way that Christ followers saw the world. This shows me that believers of these times were open to God's supernatural work—even expectant of it. Just like today's Pentecostal believers, they trusted that God could work in amazing ways in our world.

THE SPIRIT IN THE MIDDLE AGES

As the church progressed past its earliest centuries, the culture and outlook of its people were still open to the miraculous. Some of this was superstition, of course, but other aspects of it pointed more directly to the Lord. Over time, though, the most holy aspects of God's work seemed to be increasingly reserved for a more limited group. Priests, saints, and other enlightened individuals are those most often remembered this way. Though more limited, the lives of this more focused set of individuals still reveal a bent towards the miraculous.

Christian mysticism is defined by scholar Bernard McGinn as "that part, or element, of Christian belief and practice that concerns the preparation for, the consciousness of, and the effect of … a direct and transformative presence of God."[3] Mystics throughout the life of the church, notably in the Middle Ages, testified to powerful spiritual experience, visions, and insights gained as they sought the presence of God and strived toward union with him. Their testimonies—strange as they may seem at times—sound much like the encounters Pentecostals have with the Spirit. Not only that, but they could have powerful effects, too.

Consider, for instance, Julian of Norwich, a female mystic of the fourteenth and fifteenth centuries who became a respected spiritual authority. In the Eastern Church, Symeon—who lived in the tenth and eleventh centuries—shared his experiences with God and sought the spiritual gifts. Though controversial, his eventual sainthood and title "the New Theologian" speaks to the power of his testimony and teaching.

One of the most famous and well-known of the medieval saints is also one whose life testified to a transformative encounter with God in a way that might be familiar to a Pentecostal believer—Francis of Assisi. While praying one day in a broken-down old church, Francis found himself looking at a crucifix. As he did so, Jesus spoke to him from the cross and commanded him to "repair my church." Originally taking this to mean repairing the building in which he prayed, Francis later discovered the true breadth of the call he had received. It was a charge and a mission that was to have impact on the entire body of Christ. Indeed, Francis' life was seen to be so powerfully tied to the heart of Christ that he is said to have miraculously received the very wounds of Jesus, the stigmata.

A second episode told of Francis' life is further illustrative. In this story, Francis happened to see a leprous individual on the road. Repulsed by the sight of the sickened and potentially contagious individual, he kept moving. Not long after, he felt convicted for his failed nerves and returned to embrace the leper. However, upon kissing the diseased person, the object of his embrace disappeared. For Francis, this seemed evidence enough of the divine origin of his experience.

A REFORMING SPIRIT

Stories like these throughout the course of church history point towards an awareness of God's power and the place of our experience. Moving past the Middle Ages to the Reformation of the sixteenth century, Martin Luther was no stranger to the place of emotional and spiritual experience. Though an opponent of groups who sought to take the freedoms of the Reformation too far (one of which was referred to as the "Zwickau prophets"), he too experienced a powerful conversion to faith in which he describes,

"I was altogether born again and had entered paradise itself through open gates. There a totally other face of the entire Scripture showed itself to me. Thereupon I ran through the Scriptures from memory... the work of God, that is, what God does in us, the power of God, with which he makes us strong, the wisdom of God, with which he makes us wise, the strength of God, the salvation of God, the glory of God."[4]

Evocative and emotive, experiences of faith like this were absent neither for Luther nor in the Reformation of the sixteenth century.

If space allowed, we could also talk about those who took the Reformation Movement to greater extremes. Believers belonging to what historians call the Radical Reformation were freer from tradition and more open to what they understood to be the work and illumination of the Spirit. While certain of their adherents took this too far, from them we also derive key ideas about believers' baptism, the disentangling of the church from the control of the state, and holy separation from the world. Mennonites, Quakers, the Amish, and others are groups that have spiritual connection to these Reformation-era faithful.

In the generations after the Reformation, certain believers sought to codify and structure the teachings of Luther and others. Though done for legitimate reasons, some felt this emphasis on "right belief" was making faith more about facts than the experience of trust to which Luther and others testified. So, it was that during the 1600s, a group of believers emerged who began emphasizing what they considered to be the true heart of faith. Known as the Pietists, the group upheld the place of one's personal experience of faith, conversion, and the work of God to transform a person. As with other aspects of church history, this emphasis on experience is deeply reminiscent of Pentecostal emphases.

WESLEY AND BEYOND

Pietist teachings influenced none other than John Wesley, the famous English revivalist of the eighteenth century. Born in a pastor's home, Wesley eventually began training for the ministry. His initial efforts in this direction were not overly successful, however. Wesley's missionary work in the American colonies ended in relative failure. Upon his return home to England, he considered the testimony of some Moravian Pietists he had encountered beforehand. During his travels to the colonies two years earlier, his ship had faced a great storm. Despite the potentially deadly tempest, a group of Moravians on board seemed unfazed and continued singing to the Lord. Their heartfelt trust and testimony left a deep impression on the young minister.

After returning to England, Wesley at one point attended a Moravian meeting where he experienced God in such a way that he felt his heart "strangely warmed." Moving forward, Wesley began the journey towards becoming the powerful revivalist preacher for which history remembers him. Innumerable believers would come both to faith and to a deeper walk with God through Wesley's many years of teaching, preaching, and ministry. Through him, the Spirit would come to "strangely warm" many more hearts.

In North America, the same broad revival in which John Wesley participated is now sometimes referred to as the "Great Awakening." During this revival in the American colonies, leaders like Jonathan Edwards, George Whitefield, and others encouraged people to seek the new birth of conversion. Testimonies of this experience and its connection to the emotions—what Edwards called the "religious affections"—were important features of the revival.

Because of the colonial Awakening, the idea of "revival" as a vital aspect of Christian faith took root in what would become the United States. When the Second Great Awakening of the early to mid-1800s arrived, it became cemented as a deeply American phenomenon. Beginning as early as 1801 in Cane Ridge, Kentucky, a new series of revivals started that were to transform the young American republic and its people. At Cane Ridge, thousands gathered to hear preaching, to participate in worship, and to pray over the course of a week. As participants experienced the power of God, one witness described seeing "sinners dropping down on every hand, shrieking, groaning, crying for mercy, convoluted … [believers] praying, agonizing, fainting, falling down in distress for sinners, or in raptures of joy! Some singing, some shouting, clapping their hands, hugging and even kissing, laughing; others talking to the distressed, to one another, or to opposers of the work, and all this at once."[5]

Experiences like those at Cane Ridge—though not always as extreme—would mark the frontier revival culture and help transform and Christianize the American people. To contemporary

Pentecostals, such occurrences cannot help but feel familiar. They too, are a part of our story.

Further, because of the massive transformation and spread of vital Christianity into the hearts and lives of Americans, many began connecting the new passion for righteousness in their hearts with a passion to transform the country. Mission and reform were the order of the day. As revival continued, groups like the American Bible Society, the American Missionary Society, the Women's Christian Temperance Union, and the American Anti-Slavery Society came together. Looking to enact the petition of the Lord's Prayer for God's will to be done "on Earth as it is in Heaven," they sought by the power of God to reform society and prepare the way for a new era.

During the same era, this revival focus also combined with a desire for a deeper Christian life. As time went on, camp meetings emerged not just for evangelizing or reviving the faith, but also for seeking holiness as a "second work" of God's grace. Looking to go to the next level in their spiritual walk, many believers pressed in to receive this blessing. In some ways, this natural outgrowth of a revival movement had roots in the experience of Wesley and others. If his heart could be "strangely warmed" and impel him forward, so too might others look for a new experience that would alter the trajectory of their walk with God.

In the Holiness churches of the later nineteenth century, this new focus connected well with the traditional evangelical witness to salvation in Christ. These ideas also became linked with the experience of divine healing. Though miraculous occurrences were always a part of the church's testimony throughout the ages, the focus upon healing was especially pronounced during this time. Healing evangelists went forward in the power of God to proclaim victory over sickness and point to the availability of the miraculous in the present day.

To these three emphases was added an increasing belief in the premillennial return of Christ. Though a number of Christians during the later 1800s began to turn in this direction, amongst certain groups, this end-time emphasis combined with teachings on physical healing, the possibility of a deeper life in Christ, and spiritual salvation. Proudly proclaiming the "full gospel" nature of their faith, they felt that God was in the midst of their work and efforts. Holiness leader A. B. Simpson's work The Four-Fold Gospel is but one example of this. In a third edition printed in 1890, chapter titles include, "Christ Our Saviour", "Christ Our Sanctifier", "Christ Our Healer", and "Christ Our Coming Lord."[6]

Before long, many Holiness churches like these would enter into the historic Pentecostal revivals of the early twentieth century. Their story—like everything I have shared here—is also a part of our story. In the next chapter, I will point specifically to God's work within the lives of Pentecostal believers and beyond. For now, though, I hope that you have been able to gain an appreciation for the way in which God's transformative and empowering Spirit has worked through human experience and emotion, as well as in the miraculous and supernatural over the course of many centuries. This has been a part of God's mission—directly into believers' lives and through them to the world.

Christians in many different places and times have been open to God's work in their lives and emotions. Though the sustained nature of their collective experiences has not always been as intense or well-remembered as it has been in and amongst Pentecostals of our day, God's power has nonetheless been present with effect. From the days of the New Testament to the early twentieth century, the story we share has persisted. Where their journey meets the Pentecostal revival is the task to which we now turn.

CHAPTER FIVE
FALLING FIRE, BURNING HEARTS

IT TOOK ALMOST 1900 YEARS, but we have finally arrived: the history of the modern Pentecostal movement. It is a truly remarkable story, and one to which I have devoted a substantial amount of my attention as a scholar, teacher, and minister. Like many of you reading this book, this story is mine, it is ours, and it is powerful. In this chapter, we will be looking at one of the most remarkable expansions and developments in the Christian faith since perhaps the first few centuries after Christ.

For most Pentecostals, the Azusa Street Revival of 1906 is a familiar "founding moment." The move of God in Los Angeles during that season was indeed transformative. First, though, it is worth considering how even that heralded moment was not the very beginning of the Pentecostal revival. We have already looked into the revivals of the 1800s, and for good reason. These same Holiness-inspired movements emphasizing salvation, healing, the Holy Spirit, and the return of Christ would be the fertile ground out of which a new Spirit-empowered Christianity emerged.

As we saw in the last chapter, believers both in the United States and elsewhere were seeking a deeper experience with God in the years surrounding the turn of the twentieth century. Even before Azusa Street captured the attention of many, other notable revivals were taking place. One can point here to the Welsh Revival of 1904-1905

57

or developments at the Mukti Mission in India beginning in 1905. Both have been described as part of the same powerful movement of God that was beginning to sweep the world. Leading Pentecostal historian Allan Anderson writes about Indian leader Pandita Ramabai, who was "significant in both the origins of Pentecostalism and in its acceptance among the wider Christian community."[7]

Around the same time those revivals were developing, a man named Charles Parham was at work in Kansas. Ministering in the late 1800s, Parham embraced Holiness revivalism and looked for a deeper work of God in the lives of Christians. Along the way, he became extremely interested in understanding the way in which Holy Spirit baptism operated in the life of the believer. Eventually, he came to the conclusion that the "Bible evidence" of being baptized in the Holy Spirit was the same as in the second chapter of Acts: speaking in tongues. Students at a school he founded in Topeka agreed with his conclusion, and they began in earnest to seek to receive this new baptism.

Before long, they testified that one of them, Agnes Ozman, was baptized in the Holy Spirit with the evidence of speaking in tongues on January 1, 1901. By a certain reckoning, that very day was also the beginning of the twentieth century. It is fitting, then, that this new revival marks an important starting point for a one hundred-year period in which it would grow beyond all imagination.

Parham and his fellow believers understood Spirit baptism to have to do with empowerment and mission. "In the close of an age," he wrote, "God proposes to send forth men and women preaching in languages they know not a word of, which when interpreted the hearers will know is truly a message from God, spoken lips of clay by the power of the Holy Ghost."[8] The group held these two ideas together so fervently that the tongues experience they embraced during the initial revival was understood to be specifically missionary. Let me explain. Today, most Pentecostals see speaking in tongues as a kind of heavenly or spiritual language that most often has no human parallel. In most cases, we do not believe that when we speak in tongues, we utter words in Latin, German, Hindi, or other international languages.

However, for those gathered in Kansas (and later elsewhere), they trusted that God had gifted them with tongues so that they could leave for the mission field and preach almost immediately. For example, it is said that Agnes Ozman, remembered as the first person to speak in tongues at Parham's school, was gifted with the Chinese language, and a document states that she was able to write in Chinese.

As time would tell, however, many new Pentecostals who sought tongues as a missionary shortcut to language school would realize they were mistaken as to the purpose of the spiritual gift. While testimonies exist of speakers of other languages hearing a message in tongues at a service and recognizing it as their native language, instances also occurred in which Pentecostals appear to have misunderstood what the Spirit was doing in their lives.

Despite the disappointment felt in this misreading of the revival, the emphasis on missions that came along with it persisted and remains to this day an important part of Pentecostal identity. Being baptized in the Holy Spirit meant not just tongues and spiritual experience but also motivation, power, and preparation for mission and service. This linked nicely with the Pentecostal understanding of God's work in the world before Christ's return in the last days. This "latter rain" outpouring of the Spirit was a sign and a gift. The goal was evangelization of the world by means of spiritual power.

Parham's band of believers stayed relatively small, but his influence in one person's life in particular was key. While teaching in Houston a few years after the initial revival in Kansas, Parham encountered a preacher by the name of William Seymour. Seymour was African-American, born in Louisiana in 1870 to parents who were former slaves. By the time Parham encountered Seymour's teachings in 1905, Seymour had embraced the Holiness revival message as a preacher.

Seymour was interested in learning from the white Charles Parham, but because of existing ideas on race and segregation, he was unable to sit in on the teaching with others. This was no problem for Seymour, though—he simply sat outside the class and listened in as Parham unpacked his understanding of Spirit baptism and the place of tongues as evidence of God's work.

After transitioning to Los Angeles in 1906, Seymour began preaching at a Holiness church led by Pastor Julia Hutchins. His words about the Pentecostal experience of tongues were not well received by church leaders, however. Barred from their pulpit, he and some followers began holding meetings in a home. It was there, in April 1906, that Seymour and others first began to speak in tongues. Their meetings at the house on Bonnie Brae Street attracted a number of interested individuals. Notably for the time, this included a racial and ethnic mix of whites, blacks, and Hispanic individuals. Existing customs and prejudices, it seems, did not stand in light of what participants felt they were receiving from the hand of God.

A somewhat ramshackle warehouse in a Los Angeles business district, the new home of their revival at 312 Azusa Street, proved perfect for late-night services. Services and meetings there contained many of the worship practices now familiar to Pentecostals. People sang and preached, of course. Seymour was the leader of Azusa, though he was not always the one sharing the Word. Sometimes he would simply be praying on his own. Speaking in tongues was heard as people increasingly experienced the work of the Spirit as the revival continued. Interpretations and other utterances were also present.

Dancing, undergoing deep spiritual trances, and singing in the Spirit—all these and more were a part of the Azusa experience. It was, all at once, similar to yet different from various aspects of revivalism and Christian experience over the centuries. In the new Pentecostal arrangement, they were all united in the midst of a singular focus:

the baptism and work of the Holy Spirit in and amongst the people of God.

While interracial gatherings are normal in the twenty-first century, this aspect of the Azusa Street meetings would have concerned many people of the time. Seymour, of course, was an African-American, but the congregation that he led was mixed. Blacks, whites, and some Hispanics gathered at 312 Azusa Street to worship, pray, and seek the Spirit together. The desire for more of God seemed to overwhelm and transcend worldly concerns for order and segregation. Frank Bartleman, writing about Azusa some years later, famously remembered that there "the 'color line' was washed away in the blood of Christ."[9] Though this racial integration did not persist amongst all Pentecostals in coming decades, its presence near the very beginning of the revival is notably encouraging. It speaks to a work and goal of the Spirit beyond simple experience.

At Azusa and elsewhere in the early Pentecostal revival, missions was central. The general feeling was that God was intentionally pouring out his Spirit. Revivals like Azusa were all about preparing for the soon return of Christ. The urgency of that late hour and the power of the Spirit combined to motivate believers to preach the gospel everywhere.

Early in the revival, William Seymour said the following: "Let us lift up Christ to the world in all His fullness, not only in healing and salvation from all sin, but in His power to speak all the languages of the world… [we] ought to preach all of it, justification, sanctification, healing, the baptism with the Holy Ghost, and signs following… God is now confirming His word by granting signs and wonders to follow the preaching of the full gospel in Los Angeles."[10] Words like these as well as reports of Azusa and other national and international revivals printed in the pages of Seymour's newspaper, *The Apostolic Faith*, helped communicate the revival to many curious readers.

Some even traveled to Los Angeles in order to experience firsthand what God was doing. Not only that, but having been so blessed, some of these same individuals went out to be leaders in the Pentecostal movement. Charles H. Mason, the leader of what would become the largest African-American Pentecostal denomination, was transformed by his encounter at Azusa Street. G. B. Cashwell, who would later take the message of Pentecost to the American South, came to Azusa and overcame his racial prejudice to embrace the integrated prayers and ministry. William Durham, who would become an influential leader in the Midwest, was also present. Another individual, Thomas Ball Barratt, was influenced by Azusa Street before returning home to Europe where, in years to come, he would be a leading figure in the Pentecostal revival.

The missionaries that went out from Azusa Street also powerfully reflected this international aspect. Once again, the work of the Spirit in the Pentecostal revival was tightly connected with the mission of God in the world. Two of these notable individuals were Alfred Garr and his wife Lillian. Filled with the Spirit and blessed to speak in tongues, they felt called to preach the gospel in India. Just like that, they prepared to go and left for India.[11] Theirs is not a solitary story, however, as dozens of missionaries have been said to be sent out from Los Angeles around the globe, all in the power of the Spirit. This, in many ways, was just one of the assumed results of this new blessing.

As I have shown in this chapter and implied in the previous one, Azusa was not the only starting point for the Pentecostal movement. The Pentecostal movement did not simply arise out of nowhere. God was at work in a number of other places and at many different times. However, Azusa is a center of the revival, and an important one at that. It is also illustrative of many aspects of what the Holy Spirit was doing, both at that time and in the decades since.

Those who took part in the revival felt they were experiencing a new work of God that had transformative potential. They embraced the Spirit with fervor and responded in ways that showed how overwhelmed they were. More important than turn-of-the-century propriety, racial barriers, or a desire for positive press, they simply followed as they were led. If Pentecostal historian Allan Anderson is correct when he writes that the revival "is above all else a missionary movement,"[12] then few places are better to see it than in Azusa and its aftermath. The baptism of the Holy Spirit was not simply a celebration of experience, but it was tied deeply to the calling of God to evangelize the world.

The heyday of the Los Angeles revival did not last forever. Whether starting from Azusa or elsewhere around the globe, the message of Pentecost had spread. Missionaries in the United States and other locations operated in the Holy Spirit-empowered work of the gospel, indigenous believers encountered Christ in ways unique to their cultural settings, and the work went forward.

As the Pentecostal revival grew and matured, groups of churches gathered in denominational structures for mutual benefit and support. Some, like the Church of God in Christ, entered into the movement as pre-existing structures. Others, like the Assemblies of God, organized themselves for the first time in order to better accomplish the mission to which they were called. The Church of God in Cleveland, Tennessee; the International Church of the Foursquare Gospel; and others were a part of this trend. Others remained independent and never fully organized, yet went forth all the same to engage in the work at hand.

Speaking in tongues, experiencing embodied forms of worship, having holistic encounters with God—all these and more continued to be vital aspects of the Pentecostal experience. Yet, at the same time, so too was action. Evangelism, experiences of healing, and missions were all a part of this. Far from simply luxuriating in their spiritual experiences, early Pentecostals knew they had work to do. This may be part of what historian Grant Wacker describes evocatively as Pentecostals' "lightning in a bottle."[13] A combination of piety and pragmatism—or passion and action, as I might adjust the direction of Wacker's thought—is indicative of what the Pentecostal project entailed.

Early on, Pentecostals had the sense that the work the Spirit was engaged in had another mission as well: the blessing of the worldwide church. If the revival was taking place because of the soon return of Jesus, then it stood to reason that the Spirit's mission would involve the potential for all Christians to embrace this latter-day work. Sadly, however, history did not sort itself out in this way, and not long after the initial revivals, many Pentecostals found themselves unwelcome in their former congregations and derided in media and popular conception.

A MOVEMENT SPREADS AT MID-CENTURY

Though Spirit-filled growth continued around the world and in the United States, American Pentecostals for the first decades of their existence were simply not welcome in polite society. In spite of such difficulties, those who embraced the Spirit's work in their lives were no wilting flowers; they simply kept on going. They spread the word in camp meetings and rural revivals, in urban centers, and in international settings both as missionaries and as indigenous believers. Pentecostals, as they embraced the power of God, would not be deterred. Therefore, just beneath the surface of mid-century faith, the movement grew by hundreds of thousands in the United States and around the world. Pentecostalism may have been in the proverbial wilderness, but it was by no means fading away.

By 1943, none other than the Assemblies of God became a founding member of the National Association of Evangelicals. In 1958, Life magazine featured an article that went so far as to refer to the Pentecostal movement as a "third force"[14] in world Christianity, alongside Roman Catholic and Protestant churches. Clearly, the few decades of the Spirit's work and mission had yielded results.

The growth and, with increased numbers, influence of Pentecostalism had an important effect upon its reach and influence. As indicated by the Life magazine "third force," Christians outside of Pentecostal circles were beginning to take notice of what was happening. People like President John Mackay of Princeton Seminary, a former Presbyterian missionary in Latin America, began to wonder at the still-young revival. Others involved in the World Council of Churches were interested in conversation and dialogue with representatives of the movement.

Into this situation entered a South African immigrant to the United States named David du Plessis. A Pentecostal minister who believed deeply in the Spirit's work and mission, he felt compelled by God to share with other Christians about the Holy Spirit's work. As he later recalled the story, those he met at the New York offices of the World Council of Churches welcomed him. Conversations continued, and along the way, he was able to share the Pentecostal witness to other believers that he felt needed to hear and embrace what the Spirit was doing.

In the 1950s, this high-level interest in Pentecostalism took place at the same time as a more widespread and popular movement. Sometimes referred to as the Salvation-Healing Revival, it featured numerous Pentecostal evangelists and faith healers who held mass meetings in the United States and elsewhere. Their influence and reach in the post-World War II era helped make the Pentecostal experience more accessible and at times mainstream; for it was not only the Spirit-filled faithful who would attend such meetings, but also others who were in need of a healing touch.

This last bit is in many ways the story of my home church in southern New Jersey. There, a small group of German immigrants were living their lives as somewhat nominal Lutherans. One family leader, though, had some health issues. He heard about a healing meeting, led by evangelist Oral Roberts, taking place in nearby Philadelphia. Traveling to the city, they met a young Pentecostal pastor who began to minister to them. Before long, regular house meetings were taking place in the small New Jersey community, and an Assemblies of God church was founded.

As the 1960s progressed, work like David du Plessis's with church leaders and the increased reach and exposure of the healing evangelists helped usher in a new Spirit-centered revival. Often referred to as the charismatic movement or "second-wave" Pentecostalism, this new work can be understood as a continuation of the Holy Spirit's mission begun earlier in the century.

Pentecostal Episcopalians, Pentecostal Presbyterians, and Pentecostal Catholics—all these and more—worshiped in the Spirit, spoke in tongues, and were empowered by God. Called "charismatics," these Christ followers had roles to play in their churches and in the larger world. Emboldened and energized in their faith, they also embraced this broad work of the Spirit as a sign that God was bringing the church together in unity.

Although many during the time of the charismatic movement felt that the Spirit had transcended and potentially healed division, denominations persisted. Even so, the reach of the Pentecostal experience grew. In the 1980s, some pointed to a "third wave" revival amongst evangelicals who saw the power of the Holy Spirit as essential for missions and power encounters. This movement, focused on signs and wonders, understood that the miraculous work of God was important for evangelization.

At this time in history, more than at any other time, there was an exceedingly widespread sense that the Christian faith centered on the works of the Holy Spirit. Even worship styles in American Christianity tended, it seems, to take on a more emotive and expressive quality. Pentecostal perspectives have convinced many people—if not of our theology, then at least of the importance—of the heart in our Christian faith.

THE HOLY SPIRIT TODAY AND TOMORROW

On another level, one might also point to the numerical growth of the Pentecostal movement in the United States as evidence of its reach. Indeed, we have moved up the ranks! Today, less than 120 years before our earliest beginnings, three of the top fifteen largest Protestant denominations in the United States are Pentecostal.[15] Pentecostals are members of the National Association of Evangelicals. Pentecostals have been members of Presidential Cabinets. In recent years, a Pentecostal has even been featured as a major party candidate for Vice President of the United States. Pentecostal forms of faith are also featured prominently by means of church groups like Hillsong and popular speakers like Judah Smith, T.D. Jakes, Joyce Meyer, and many other ministers with a wide audience who are representatives of the Pentecostal revival.

With such developments in the United States, one might be tempted to think that our shared story is one of victory only. While such a temptation clearly has evidence to commend it, questions exist in our contemporary era. One of these has to do with power and respectability. Now that we have "arrived" as a movement and have gained more access to the main stage, so to speak, it is tempting for Pentecostals to want to be more "respectable" in the public eye. For some, more extreme revival forms and expressions of the Spirit need not apply.

Such desires are born not only of pride and embarrassment at not being more "normal" in the popular eye, but also of a desire to share the gospel with outsiders we feel might be put off by tongues, prophecy, or emotional prayer services. Missionality, it seems, may come into conflict with Pentecostalism. In the midst of such concerns, we begin to doubt ourselves. The Pentecostal movement has become diffused, yes. However, in that diffusion, what is the place of its passionate focus on the power of the Spirit? I alluded to these same concerns in an earlier chapter. As a Pentecostal believer, minister, and historian, they continue to demand my focus.

Questions about identity for Pentecostals in the United States is further heightened when we look around the world. For as much as our story in the United States has been one of growth and development, our Pentecostal sisters and brothers around the globe have experienced this to an even greater degree. As recently as 2010, it was possible to speak of over 585 million "renewalists" (Pentecostal types) around the globe. Asia has 125 million, Latin America boasts 180 million, and Africa claims over 175 million fellow believers who are embracing the work of the Spirit.[16]

Pentecostals and those of similar faith perspectives may now represent, by some counts, nearly twenty-five percent of the over two billion Christians around the world. In many of these areas, observing indigenous expressions of faith is like looking back at the earlier chapters of the American Pentecostal story. Exorcisms, healings, signs, wonders, extended prayer services, revival meetings, spiritual warfare, and visions—you name it, and our fellow sisters and brothers are embracing these experiences. As they do, they are growing. In their faith, a passionate abandon in the Spirit connects with a passionate abandon for souls.

Parts of the Pentecostal story, like those taking place outside the United States, can leave us wondering not only about the past and present, but also about our future. If we and our African counterparts are representatives of twenty-first century Pentecostals, what binds us together? How are we the same? How is our story a shared one? Are we missing something, and do we need to jettison our modern-day trapping for more "old-time religion"? These questions and more can haunt us, but they are vital for us to consider.

We know that our movement was born out of a desire for something more—more of God and his power. Nevertheless, as contemporary American Pentecostals, we are sometimes caught enjoying the emotional aspects of our faith in worship and desiring to be respectable or accepted by society and those we wish to evangelize.

All the while, we may be feeling guilty that we are not living up to the "true Pentecost" of our past and the passions of the larger global movement even now. For good reason, we might ask ourselves what a Pentecostal really is. To truly live in the Spirit, need it look like it did in the third century, the time of Saint Francis, a revival in 1906, or a mass meeting in sub-Saharan Africa in 2017? Alternatively, in the calmer and more secular religious climate of the United States, is the age of expressive spirituality or revivalistic Pentecostal expression no longer the way to go?

As I look at our shared narrative in both the past and present, I cannot help but recall my modified version of Bonhoeffer's famous query: "Who is the Holy Spirit, for us, today?" Our answer to this question—a question that is deeply lodged in the story of the Christian faith and the Pentecostal testimony—is one with which we must struggle.

We believe that God is acting through the Holy Spirit to do important work today. It is work that, while connected to our experience, goes far beyond it and is as deeply Pentecostal as it is focused upon the mission of God. In the next chapter, therefore, we will begin to consider the elusive term missional as a means to comprehend this vital reality.

CHAPTER SIX

WHAT IS MISSIONAL?

PICTURE THE SCENE. You are in a room of enterprising pastors and church planters gathered from around the country to pray together, learn from each other, and strategize how best to engage in ministry in the twenty-first century. Big-name leaders are prepared to address them, and they are ready to learn how best to succeed in ministry, see souls saved, and grow their churches.

They are meeting in a huge church, Chick-fil-A is catering the lunch, and the musical worship team is well known around the country. The pastors gathered are an interdenominational bunch from a variety of evangelical and Pentecostal backgrounds, and they are ready for that elusive "next step" in the ministry to which God has called them.

What specifically has attracted them to this moment? After all, numerous pastors' conferences are available. What motivates them to come here? A certain number felt clearly led by the Lord to attend. For some, it was the slate of speakers. Of course, the fact that the conference was held in a warm and sunny location in the dead of winter did not hurt. Most of the motivation behind those in attendance, however, was due to the title of the conference: "Being a Missional Church."

"Missional". You have heard the word. We all have. For the past decade or longer, it has been rather trendy in the church world to describe what we are doing as "being missional." We want to talk about mission. We want to be "on mission." Although it is a new way of phrasing what we take to be an old idea, we have grasped onto missionality as a way forward in our complex age. The pastors gathered at this conference resonate with its stated theme for many of these reasons. They want to connect what they are doing with a sense of purpose and direction. They desire to reach the culture and are looking for the means to do so.

What does "missional" actually mean? What is it, beyond a mere buzzword or a term so broad that we can fill it with whatever meaning we want? Is it just a trend, or is it something deeper and more valuable? Just the idea itself was important enough to attract dozens of people to our hypothetical pastors' conference. What stands behind it in real life is a veritable clearinghouse of all that is missional. Books, conferences, seminars, strategies, college courses, graduate programs—you name it—are all connected to the term. Try Google searching it, and you will find over 1.8 million hits.

That is enormous weight on just one word.

It is our (Don's and my) assertion that being missional is indeed a vital aspect of Christianity. It is so popular for good reason. However—and this is important—we also feel that the way that people interpret or practice the term and the idea can often be a little "off target."

What we hope to accomplish in this chapter, therefore, is fourfold: 1) to unpack what we often (and potentially incorrectly) mean when we use the term, 2) to provide some biblical context for understanding the background of the concept of being "missional", 3) to explain some theological and practical definitions, and 4) to make a strong case for why missionality is not just helpful, but essential to living for Jesus.

I realize I am stating the obvious, but it is important to keep in mind that the term "missional" derives in part from the concept of "mission". In the same way, it is related, in our Christian understanding, to the missionary world. I will briefly touch on some of these concepts later, but for now it is enough to say that missionary reflection on Christianity in Western culture in the second half of the twentieth century was an important catalyst of missional thinking. By the time Darrell Guder published *The Missional Church: A Vision for the Sending of the Church in North America* in 1998, the pump was primed for the upsurge of interest in all that is missional in the decades that followed.

If being missional is imperative, I once again return to the question, what is it? Ask a different person on a different day, and you might just get a different answer. This tricky word has an unfortunately generous definition. Too many meanings muddy the waters, in the process making it difficult to have valid conversation. So, then, what might we mean when we say that we are being missional, and do those potential definitions withstand?

One option for interpreting the word "missional" is to connect it closely to our understanding of missionaries. In Pentecostal circles, after all, we are all about missionaries. As churches, we support international workers all across the globe who spread the word of Jesus to all nature of people groups. As individuals, many of us have a missionary or two to which we financially donate every month. We read missionary reports, hear them speak in our churches, and are encouraged by the work they do in preaching the gospel. As a church, we might even sponsor fundraising efforts for missionary equipment or vehicles. Some of us even go on short-term mission trips to Central America, Asia, or Africa.

This kind of focus on missionary efforts is significant, for in it we are looking to support the Great Commission's command to "Go therefore and make disciples of all nations…" (Matthew 28:19). From a certain point of view, then, we are partnering with those on a mission and orienting our churches—and our hearts—in a missionary or what we might call a "missional" direction. If being missional is primarily a stance or position out of which we act, then surely being involved with missionaries is "missional".

Okay, we think, missionaries are by definition "missional", and therefore, we get to consider ourselves missional by being their supporters in prayer, finances, or short-term trips, right? From a certain point of view, that makes sense. Nevertheless, considered in another way, we might stop and wonder whether that is really meant to encompass the full breadth of what is involved in being missional. Reflecting a little more deeply about the passions and sacrifices that motivate the international missionaries we look to as heroes, we may begin to wonder if God is calling us to more.

Looking again to the Great Commission (notice the word "mission" again), we are reminded that the call to make disciples is not just something for us to support in other people's lives and ministries. It is a call for *all* Christians. We have good news to share, and it is contingent upon us to share it. "Missional", we assume then, means evangelism. This can take numerous forms, but it is always with the goal of helping people realize the salvation available to them in Jesus Christ.

In the lead-up to Christmas and Easter, our congregation engages in a massive campaign to bring our friends and neighbors to church. We are a part of a small group that helps us better explain and defend our faith to those who do not believe. These are but two ways in which we can engage as we embrace missional living as evangelism. On a personal level, evangelism might involve prayer that co-workers and friends come to know Christ. For others in our congregation, this kind of missionality might involve evangelizing door-to-door or passing out gospels or gospel tracts. Those bolder souls in our midst might go to public areas and street corners to engage in preaching efforts directed at the many lost sheep in our world.

If some of these evangelistic efforts seem a bit intense to you, please understand that I am not saying that these are the only ways to evangelize. I am simply trying to describe what we might picture when we think about sharing our faith as a way to be missional. The Pentecostal story is filled with all of these methods and more, as women and men embracing God's call to evangelize have gone forth to do just that.

This mission to evangelize is embraced so that people will hear the loving message of God in Christ and come to faith in him. Moving from a state of being lost and separate from God, evangelism helps sinners (and indeed, we are all sinners) understand that the grace of God awaits all who accept his Son. In what is perhaps the most well-known verse in all of Scripture, Jesus says it perfectly: "For God so loved the world that he gave his one and only Son, that whoever believes in him shall not perish but have eternal life" (John 3:16). We are people with good news, and we have a mission to share it. This is mission oriented, certainly, but is this the extent of being missional?

At the church level, when we think about evangelism and mission, we are—not surprisingly—concerned with more than simply getting people to cross the line of faith and put their trust in Christ. While this is foundational and essential, we also believe it is only the beginning of one's walk with God. The development of believers as lifelong disciples, who in turn share their faith with and develop future believers, is all a part of this ongoing mission. As such, we believe churches—local congregations—have an important role to play in this process.

It is not surprising that in the past few decades, most churches have embraced the idea that they should have a mission or vision statement to guide their life and actions. Sometimes these statements are rather detailed; other times they are brief and easy to memorize. No matter their shape, they are meant to be definitive statements concerning what the congregation is about and to what mission God has called them in their unique context. They provide identity and purpose for local churches, guiding our collective actions. In that they are mission-focused documents, surely, they must be a sign that we are being missional, right?

Sort of.

Like each of the other items discussed here, having a

congregational mission statement is helpful, and many deeply biblical mission statements exist. At the same time, having a church
mission statement—even a really good one—does not mean that
we are embracing the full sense of what being missional might be.
Moreover, the location of a mission statement within the center of the
life of the congregation can have the unintended effect of making it
all about what our local church is doing. This congregationally-based
center of gravity can bend our definition towards two aspects of what
we might think "missional" means that are, more than just incom-
plete, but are also problematic.

"We need to get them to church." You have heard it before. Often
it is simple verbal shorthand for someone coming to faith in Jesus
Christ. Even so, it can indicate a subconscious understanding of what
being missional entails. We know as Christians that people need
Jesus, and we know the mission given to us by God. Furthermore,
we know that our church is a part of that mission. Naturally, we want
people to come to our church, our meeting time, or our building.
That is how we can embrace the missional call.

In a certain way, this makes sense. Our pastors and preachers
spend time in prayer and study to prepare the messages they share
during meeting times at our church. Worship leaders practice songs
based upon the Bible and theology. We feel that God is present as
we gather. More often than not, an explanation of the salvation message and an invitation to embrace it are a part of our gatherings.
Attending church is an excellent way for a person to experience all
of this and more. However, is all of this the best way to understand
what it is to be missional?

Please understand me. I love the work of the local church. I believe
in what God is doing in and amongst groups of Christ followers all
over the world. God does meet people in powerfully salvific ways in
church services. However—and this is significant—simply getting
someone to come to your meeting or building is not all it takes to be
missional. Christian gatherings can be a positive experience for sure,

but that is not the only place that God works. Getting someone to come to church with me on Sunday might make me feel like I am doing the Lord's work, but that does not mean that my responsibility for Christ and his mission end there. Having our neighbors cross the threshold of a church building on Sunday at 11 a.m. is not, in other words, the finish line.

Focusing on "getting people to church" is therefore understandable shorthand for being missional, even as it falls woefully short of our calling as Christians. Even so, because we can celebrate this tangible accomplishment—either individually or corporately—it can tend to become a less-than-helpful benchmark. While God can and does accomplish much in and through our churches, if we are focusing our missional energy simply on this, we may miss something important.

When I was a youth pastor, I joined a dozen or so other youth ministries for a combined winter retreat each February. During one of them, our evening speaker was encouraging students to gather around the altar for prayer and worship. One of the ways he did so continues to stick in my mind. Speaking to the crowd of a few hundred, he said something like, "Alright, everyone, are you ready? In just a moment, I'm going to count to five. When I get to five, I want all of you to come as fast as you can to this altar. Are you ready? Are you ready? Let's start. One. Two. Three. Four. FIIIIVE!" In a room full of students aged twelve through eighteen, what do you think happened? Exactly. Just about the entire room rushed up to that altar. What a moment! What a picture! All the same—what did it mean? The speaker had gotten many people to come forward, no doubt. A good deal of this, though, had more to do with enthusiasm and group psychology than some deep desire to pray at the altar. It might have looked remarkable if someone took a picture for social media. The lasting effect of the evening, though, is less clear.

If we are being brutally honest, we know that celebrating numbers and visuals like this altar call tell only a part of the story. We can try many ways to get people to come and pray at an altar or to get people to come to our churches. In many of our churches, we have become quite proficient at this latter advertising approach.

In an effort to encourage people to encounter Jesus in our church communities, we "sell" ourselves in many ways. Sometimes this simply involves good marketing—an effective use of social media, graphic design, web presence, and e-mail or direct mailings. The more we get our names out there, the better. Often these strategies are combined with events or activities meant to attract people from wherever they might be to wherever our church is, such as an Easter egg hunt, a summer sports camp, a provocatively titled sermon series, or even free food and music. If the missional goal is to get people in the doors, we will work to do what it takes. We want people to be comfortable, so in the process, we will update our style, dress code, and music to help people feel at home.

Connecting with people where they are is beneficial. Nevertheless, sometimes such good intentions have other effects on our congregations that can influence the way we practice our faith. Not all of these changes are positive. I think most notably here of Pentecostal congregations. As I have indicated in previous chapters about the history of the movement, certain traditional aspects of Pentecostal worship can be very, shall we say, "expressive".

Congregants will speak in tongues as inspired by the Holy Spirit. They will give interpretations of tongues, and they will speak words of knowledge or prophecy. All of these take place and are seen by Pentecostals as tied to the details provided by the apostle Paul in I Corinthians and elsewhere. Sometimes, so overwhelmed by what God's Spirit is doing in their midst and in their lives, Pentecostals will fall to the floor, shout, or exhibit other bodily expressions.

All of these kinds of practices testify to something powerful that God may be doing in hearts and lives. However, the outward appearance or result can be a little peculiar. I do not want to say "weird," because the word has negative connotations that I feel better not ascribing to the Holy Spirit. I will say this, though: many of the traditional modes and styles of expression in Pentecostal churches are certainly out of the ordinary.

In light of the extraordinary nature of much of this, many have wondered if traditional Pentecostalism is just "too much" to be genuinely missional. If we are trying to reach the average unchurched person, we think we need to teach them about Jesus without all the "extra" Holy Spirit stuff mixed in the middle. Moreover, would not a full-on Pentecostal revival service simply freak out some people? Sure, we believe in what God's power can do, but we are nonetheless nervous about unleashing it on the uninitiated.

In my years as a youth pastor, I felt this tension sharply. Though I am, literally, a card-carrying Pentecostal minister, I rarely tended to emphasize those doctrines as I pastored teenagers in New Jersey for six years. To be sure, I did not deny the power of the Holy Spirit, nor did I reject Pentecostalism. I just figured that all of it was too complicated (and off-putting) for students who simply needed to know Jesus. Speaking in tongues and baptism in the Holy Spirit? All this I reserved for special services or summer camp.

I suspect that many of my fellow youth pastors have felt the same way, and it is not just us. Many Pentecostal leaders, faced with the sheer task of embracing evangelism and getting people "in the doors," have purposely deemphasized the more demonstrative gifts of the Spirit in church services. After all, we want people to feel comfortable and at home. Walking into a place where numerous unexpected spiritual expressions are practiced all at once? The fear is that it is just too much.

In addition to downplaying the more Pentecostal aspects of our congregations, our desire to be missional (as we understand it) also manifests itself in the many other adjustments we make along the way. In short, we want to be "seeker sensitive." More casual dress, fewer hymns, coffee bars in the lobby, cool video announcements—you name it, and we are willing to try it. We want to reach people, right? Please hear me, though: I mention these not to reject them, but simply to show how the desire to fulfill our interpretation of missional means, "getting people in church," using whatever tools available. All these are signs of the direction in which we are headed.

You see, if the focus is only getting people to come to us, we may unintentionally be willing to make changes or compromises that give up the broader ends to which we are called just to get people to come to us. Our definition of "missional" and our commitment to it as an ideal can make us focus on much more limited ends than what God desires. In so doing, we can let go of so much without need. Especially for us Pentecostals, this can lead to the jettisoning of foundational parts of what we believe to be true about experiencing God in the power of the Holy Spirit. We (Don and I) believe this can cause us to miss what God really desires to do in and through us. This is all because of a definition of "missional" that falls short.

So then, what is "missional", really? To begin to explain this, let me tell you a story.

When I was a youth pastor, our church was housed in an old Presbyterian church in a mid-sized town in New Jersey. Every year in April, the town shut down its main street for a fair. Community groups performed, vendors sold food, and students at the local university ran various booths, one of which involved throwing whipped cream pies at college students, which I thought was rather clever.

Like other churches in town, our congregation had its own booth, which our youth ministry and other members managed. We served bottles of water, offered a face painting station, and provided church literature for anyone who was interested. We also distributed free Bibles. These were just basic paperbacks—nothing complicated or fancy—but they did have interesting covers. Calling the Bible "The Story of God," it summarized the narrative like this: "How God, having lovingly created the world and watched it turn against his purpose, lived among us, was still rejected because He didn't fit expectations, turned everything upside down to get things back on track and now invites you to find your place in the Story of God."

I know it is a bit of a run-on sentence, but it is powerful all the same. I believe that, however imperfectly, the statement on the front of that Bible begins to explain what I consider not only God's story, but God's mission as well. That, I would argue, is where our discussion of the term "missional" should begin.

To understand this story biblically, some scholars have divided the drama into a number of "acts." The first, then, is creation. Of course, we know that God creates everything good. Adam and Eve are together in Eden, God walks with them, and all is good. Enter the second act. Free will on the part of those made in God's image leads to sin—separation from God—and Eden is left behind, as the formerly close relationship God has with his people is broken. The world enters into distraught chaos.

Though the drama's third act does not fix everything, it is hopeful about other possibilities. God makes a covenant with Abraham and his descendants. Those who would become the nation of Israel are promised a special relationship with God. Amongst this new people with whom God desires to have relationship, he promises to bless all nations, all peoples, and indeed, the whole world. Israel has its difficulties holding up its end of the bargain and faces many challenges on the way. Their walk with God is no Edenic ideal, but God does remain faithful to them.

Eventually, God begins to bring his promises to all nations to fulfillment by taking on flesh in his own being and becoming incarnate in Jesus Christ. Jesus, literally "God with us", is born into humanity to teach, heal, suffer, die, and rise for us and for our salvation. His work for us in this fourth act leads to the inauguration of the fifth act in which we now live—the era of the church. Even now, we await the sixth and final act that is the final redemption of all creation at the end of time. This story, in sum, shows us God's mission spread over time. The Scripture is replete with details describing the mission of God in both the Old and New Testaments.

This "whole Bible" understanding comes together well in the accounts of Jesus' birth in the gospels. The inspired authors show that Jesus is the promised Messiah. Matthew reminds readers in 1:23 that the newborn child will be Immanuel— "God with us". He goes on to emphasize the importance of Jesus' birthplace in Bethlehem, pointing to the prophecy about how "out of you will come a ruler who will be the shepherd of my people Israel" (2:6). In the gospel of Luke, aged Simeon, who had waited years to see God's promise fulfilled, proclaims to the Lord and comments on both his story and the largest narrative of all to which Scripture had been pointing: "For my eyes have seen your salvation, which you have prepared in the sight of all people, a light for revelation to the Gentiles and for glory to your people Israel" (2:30-32).

As God in the flesh, Jesus exemplifies the mission of God through his earthly ministry. Early on, he begins calling others to follow him, telling them to drop what they are doing. He has plans that he "will make [them] fishers of men" (Mark 1:17), which is all a part of his larger goal to "seek and save the lost" (Luke 19:10). As he looks out at the world and its people, he sees people in need. Like the hungry crowd that gathers in the gospel of Mark, they are "like sheep without a shepherd" (6:34).

I could go on and on detailing the words and work of Jesus as a means of illustrating the mission of God. For now, though, two statements bear witness to the Lord's heart. The first is a passage of Scripture I mentioned earlier and which needs little introduction. Appearing near the beginning in the gospel of John, Jesus, in an encounter with a man name Nicodemus, sums up God's mission in crystal clear perfection: "For God so loved the world that he gave his one and only Son, that whoever believes in him shall not perish but have eternal life" (3:16). Succinct and memorable, it speaks to the heart, the goal, and the great story of God.

John 3:16, though, is only one place out of many in the Bible that speaks to this mission. Other passages help to deepen our understanding of it, calling to mind that while our spiritual salvation is a foundational and core end of God's work, it is not the end. I think of what is an even more foundational passage for me than John 3:16 is Luke 4. Standing up in a synagogue in Nazareth, we hear Jesus proclaim the following, and in the process, we understand that God's goals may be broader and deeper than we might sometimes imagine:

> "The Spirit of the Lord is on me, because he has anointed me to proclaim good news to the poor. He has sent me to proclaim freedom for the prisoners and recovery of sight for the blind, to set the oppressed free, to proclaim the year of the Lord's favor.

> "Then he rolled up the scroll, gave it back to the attendant and sat down. The eyes of everyone in the synagogue were fastened on him. He began by saying to them, 'Today this scripture is fulfilled in your hearing.'" (Luke 4:18-21)

Just think: in this one singular moment, Jesus talks about the many ways in which God's passion and care for his people, so loved, yet separated from him and broken in so many ways, are going to be made whole again. Jesus is beginning to enact the "year of the Lord's favor."

This year of the Lord's favor is far from a 365-day period. It is the ultimate completion of God's mission amongst us, begun in the earthly life of Jesus, carried on throughout the age of the church, and brought to completion at the end of it all. It connects with the Great "Co-mission" Christ leaves his followers—us—at the end of Matthew, "Therefore go and make disciples of all nations, baptizing them in the name of the Father and of the Son and of the Holy Spirit, and teaching them to obey everything I have commanded you" (28:19-20).

As the church is in its infancy, Paul reminds the scattered congregations to whom he writes of a goal, a purpose, and a mission to which they are called. In the midst of the still-broken world that has been "groaning as in the pains of childbirth right up to the present time" (Romans 8:22), believers have been called on a journey of service in the name of their Lord. "All this," he reminds Christ followers, "is from God, who reconciled us to himself through Christ and gave us the ministry of reconciliation: that God was reconciling the world to himself in Christ, not counting people's sins against them. And he has committed to us the message of reconciliation. We are therefore Christ's ambassadors, as though God were making his appeal through us" (II Corinthians 5:18-20).

Elsewhere, Paul writes about how "it is for freedom that Christ has set us free" (Ephesians 5:1), and that in Christ God has made us all—Jew and Gentile alike—one: "He came and preached peace to you who were far away and peace to those who were near. For through him we both have access to the Father by one Spirit" (Ephesians 2:17-18). All of this is but the beginning of the mission's ultimate aim and purpose. In the last book of the Bible, God reminds us that in the age to come, the culmination of the story of God (and us) will be in a time and place when "He will wipe every tear from [our] eyes. There will be no more death or mourning or crying or pain, for the old order of things has passed away" (Revelation 21:8). In the evocative image that Revelation provides of the New Jerusalem, the river in the city's middle has a Tree of Life on each of its sides—the same tree alive in Eden. God, in other words, brings it all back to completion.

The mission of God is to reconcile the world to himself. God has purposed that in so doing, he comes to make everything new (Revelation 21:5). He seeks the lost and offers salvation. He comforts the brokenhearted and heals wounds, both spiritual and physical. He frees prisoners of many stripes and advances his kingdom as he looks to work in and through us. All of this and more is the mission of God, and it is active in the world today. As C. S. Lewis powerfully evokes in the classic allegory of Christ in *The Lion, the Witch, and the Wardrobe*, Aslan is on the move.

If all of this is God's mission, then our being missional needs to be closely aligned with it. All too often, however, our focus on the mission falters. Experts call this "mission drift." When emphasis on any one purpose is less than clear, our corresponding actions can become muddled and ineffective. The military knows this all too well, which is why much discussion in recent years has to do with these ideas. Combatting militants and insurgents requires precision; for without any clear aim, no specific goals can be achieved. Unclear outcomes guarantee unclear results.

Though I believe the church has many reasons to avoid overly military metaphors, the idea of mission drift connects particularly well with the principle Don and I are trying to convey. Besides that, mission drift is applicable in business, personal life, and spiritual matters as well as military ones.

The term "missional" dates back at least as far as the British missionary Lesslie Newbigin (1909-1998). Reflecting on increasingly secular Western society in the middle of the twentieth century, he encouraged the church to adapt in a missionally focused way. Theologian Darrell Guder, who in 1998 published an edited volume entitled *Missional Church: A Vision for the Sending of the Church in North America*, picked up related themes. Within he writes, "The basic thesis of this book is that the answer to the crisis of the North American church will not be found at the level of method and problem solving … the problem is much more deeply rooted. It has to do with who we are and what we are for."[17] In those few words, Guder reminds us that all of our clever ideas, adaptations, and trendiness pale in comparison to the fact we are the people of a missional God, the body of Christ that is always meant to be "on mission."

Others have reflected on missional themes, in the process helping provide more definition to the term. Missiologist Alan Hirsch has said the following:

"A missional community sees the mission as both its originating impulse and its organizing principle. A missional community is patterned after what God has done in Jesus Christ. In the incarnation God sent his Son. Similarly, to be missional means to be sent into the world; we do not expect people to come to us. This posture differentiates a missional church from an attractional church."[18]

Clearly, Hirsch ties missionality to the action of God in going to the world rather than our action in getting people to come to us. Dr. Terry Minter echoes these sentiments, believing that "missional churches challenge and equip their parishioners to live as agents of God's grace outside the worship center and to become agents of Christ's mission on this earth."[19]

Clearly, being missional has to do with going to the world rather than expecting or enticing others to come to us. This is an essential feature of the whole enterprise. As Dr. Minter notes, we are "God's sent people" who are called "into the world to spread God's love among all types of needy people who are without the hope of Christ."[20] This going is essential, not just because it sounds like a good idea, but because it is deeply rooted in the heart of the God we serve. God's own actions throughout the Bible speak to a persistent mission. By God's grace, this mission is now one in which we are invited to take part.

To be on this mission means action, yes, but it also means that we understand the mission. Acting without understanding could be a futile endeavor—like the person who wants to keep busy "just because." God is a God of purpose and design, and as we act on mission, we need to do so with an understanding of what is involved. We need to search the Scripture and listen for the Spirit, discerning what is close to God's own heart. It is far too easy to embrace the idea of "going" without knowing where the destination is—a recipe for some serious mission drift.

When I think about the mission of God and what that means, I am reminded repeatedly of the passage from Luke 4 that I quoted earlier. In Jesus' proclamation of "the year of the Lord's favor," in which he "proclaim[s] good news to the poor … freedom for the prisoners and recovery of sight for the blind [and] to set the oppressed free," I see the heart of God. Such a gospel focus, centered on the action of God, helps align our mission appropriately. Our close adherence to the Bible's account of God's own Being guarantees that we do not "put the cart before the horse," following our own desires first and only then inviting God to come and join us. Rather, it truly allows us to follow Christ and be on God's mission.

To be "missional" means to be people who are on board with nothing less than the mission of God itself—a mission modeled through the pages of the Scripture and in which God is engaged even now. Impelled by Christ's example and call to enter into a broken world, he leads us to walk in his very steps.

I began this chapter by describing a hypothetical pastors' conference. Attendees were ready and excited to learn more about the meeting's theme: "Being a Missional Church." What they—and sometimes we—fail to realize is that being missional is not about getting people to come and be a part of our congregation. It is not about growing our numbers, neither is it simply a bunch of new ways for us to evangelize. While missionality can and does intersect with these ideas at certain points, it is about something more. It is about the mission of God.

Mission is essential. Without it, we have no direction and, frankly, little sense of identity. What we do and how we live is in a very large sense deeply connected to who we are. When we live as missional Christians and churches, we follow our one true Leader who, by his grace, has allowed us to partner in mission. Such a mission is, as I have shown, written all over the pages of Scripture.

At its heart, missionality provides us with basic operating instructions and reminds us of the proper starting point in our lives of faith. Beyond modern buildings, nice mission statements, and even our own expansive dreams, we are called to be on God's mission in the midst of God's plan. In the same way that God is as God has been—at work in and amongst creation—we are called to go to a hurting world to bring life, hope, and love. Such work is never to be undertaken in our own name but always in the name of God.

Though many competing forces, trends, ideas, and schemes can assault and assail us as we consider the work of our local congregations and the plans of our individual lives, this primary mission rises above all of it. It is there, ready for us to grasp it. It is like the old television show that often repeated, "This is your mission, if you choose to accept it." In light of both the great need in our world and the deep honor of being called to partner with our Lord, I certainly hope that we do. Ultimately, being missional in this truest sense is like coming home, for it is what the Lord has had for us from the moment we were first transformed by the very same mission.

CHAPTER SEVEN

JESUS THE FIRST PENTECOSTAL

IT'S NOT LIKELY you've heard Jesus described as a Pentecostal before. It just isn't a term we often use when talking about Him. Throughout history, He has been referred to in many ways: Lord, Master, Savior, Shepherd. But Pentecostal? Not so often.

After all, the events of Acts 2 do not occur until after Jesus ascends to the Father. It is only after he departs that the Comforter is promised (John 14). Furthermore, we understand "Pentecostal" to mean a certain type of contemporary style, theology, or behavior that we do not immediately associate with Him. Jesus is certainly not a card-carrying member of the Assemblies of God or the Church of God in Christ. Nevertheless, the Bible shows Jesus to be particularly Spirit-led. As He accomplishes His mission on Earth, Jesus is the very first Pentecostal.

Since you're reading this book, I'm willing to bet that you are sold—or at least open—to the Pentecostal expression and experience of faith. In the same way, I also believe that you have more than a passing interest in what it means to be on the mission of God. And, because you've read this far, I'm sure that you are ready to hear what Don and I think these two things have to do with one another.

"Missional" and "Pentecostal" are the twin themes of this book. They belong together both in Jesus' life and in ours. We have made the case that they are vital biblical characteristics in faith and ministry. But: how exactly do they interact? Can they be a part of our experience at the same time? Or are they inevitably at odds?

This last question is perhaps the most pressing for us because, after all, we Pentecostals love our movement. We adore our Pentecostal experience. Speaking in tongues during worship, words of wisdom at the altar, church members collapsing under the power of the Spirit—all of these are traditional hallmarks we have come to embrace as part of our experience of faith. Like many of those reading this book, my heart warms at the memories of what God has done in my life. Camps, special services, the church altars of my youth—each held experiences with the Spirit that were transformative. And this is not just me. The diverse history of our movement testifies to the explosive power of God revealed in some very unusual ways.

There's a problem, however. Despite the best intentions, our Pentecostal passion runs up against another reality we often strongly embrace: missionality. A truly missional, outreach-focused church, we assume, could never abide all that Pentecostal "stuff." A missional focus often rejects the emphasis we place upon such Pentecostal activities as being distracting or detrimental to our real goals. After all, if our actions and experiences are extreme or unhelpful to outsiders, why in the world would we continue with them? From this perspective, holding on too tightly is counterproductive. The adjectives "missional" and "Pentecostal", as most commonly understood, are therefore mutually exclusive. To be one means to scrap the other, and vice versa.

As you might suspect, Don and I reject this approach. We don't think it is right. We don't think it is right or biblical. Most importantly, we don't think it is at the heart of God. Far from being competing ideas or principles in the Christian life, the Pentecostal reality and the missional call naturally and purposely belong together. In short, we believe that to be Pentecostal means to be missional. So too being missional means living into the ongoing mission of God's own Spirit—the same Spirit at work in Jesus Christ, given to the

Church at Pentecost, and which has continually renewed God's people for two millennia. Being missional, in its richest sense, means being Pentecostal. Just like Jesus.

PENTECOST AND POWER

Getting lost in Pentecostal experience without a clear mission is confusing at best and a dead end at worst. In a similar way, getting caught up in missionality without relying on God's Spirit means missing out on the power God has for the work to which He calls us. Missional Pentecostalism and Pentecostal missionality avoid these dangers by keeping two things together which ought never have been separated in the first place.

For the Pentecostal, the linkage of these two should never be very far from our minds. After all, the early chapters of the book of Acts hold them together quite well. For years Pentecostals proudly proclaimed that the Holy Spirit empowers us for witness, recalling the famous statement in Acts 1:8 that "…you will receive power when the Holy Spirit comes on you; and you will be my witnesses…" If that were not enough, consider the example of Peter. His transition from denier of Christ to Jesus' most fervent witness is interrupted significantly by the giving of the Holy Spirit at Pentecost. In that experience, Peter is changed. He embraces the mission to which he is called, and three thousand new believers are the result (Acts 2:41).

If you've spent any time in a traditional Pentecostal setting, you don't need me to tell you all this. Themes like this from the book of Acts are everywhere. I grew up in an Assemblies of God church and youth ministry, and I can tell you that this teaching was both standard and expected. The message was clear: the Holy Spirit gave Christians power and encouragement to share their faith. Sometimes the Spirit would even give us the words to say even when we didn't know. Especially when we didn't know. This was what I was taught and what I continue to believe to this day.

The lessons of the book of Acts deserve to be kept in the forefront of our faith and life. In a coming chapter, Don will walk us through some of the book's key moments. Along the way he will remind us of the power of the Spirit in action. The evidence is clear. The Holy Spirit was truly at work in the Church's earliest days as Christians went about doing what God called them to do.

In Pentecostal preaching and teaching, this connection between the power of the Spirit and a call to embrace God's mission is commonplace. But maybe it is too well known. Perhaps it has been repeated so much and we "know" it so well that we start to ignore that vital connection. And that is a dangerous place for us to be.

I struggled with something like this during my time as a young pastor. As I served our local church and its teens, there were a lot of different backgrounds represented. Some were friends of friends that had no church background. Others were young people who came to faith in their teen years. Then there were those who had grown up in the church. Sometimes these were the hardest, like the older son in the prodigal story. They had heard it all. They "knew" it all. At times, of course, I'd have to remind them of what they knew. About God. About His call on their lives. About the wisdom or foolishness of the decisions they had made or were contemplating making. In response I sometimes simply got this: "I know, Pastor Josh. I know."

In a certain sense, they were right. They did have the basic content in their heads. It had been drilled into their minds through repetition over the years. But it had grown stale, perhaps, or they had simply heard it so much that it had little meaning anymore. So when a student might say they "knew," in my heart I realized that it was only on the most "surfacey" of levels. To help them realize, understand, and embrace what they knew, they'd need to hear it in a new way. When it comes to the message of Pentecost and mission, I think we do, too.

A PENTECOSTAL SCENE IN THE LIFE OF JESUS

I have a confession to make: as powerful as the book of Acts is, for me the central biblical passage that links mission and the Holy Spirit is not there. Sure, I fully embrace the testimony of the first-century Church. But my touchstone? My center of gravity? Well, you have to look a little earlier in the Bible for that. You have to look to Jesus, the first Pentecostal.

We forget sometimes that Acts is the second volume in a two-part history that Luke is writing. The gospel that bears his name comes first. As you would expect from the same author, repeated themes appear in both books. One of these, unsurprisingly, is the Holy Spirit. As a matter of fact, the moment I want to draw our attention to in Luke is just one of these times. It reinforces what we see in Acts 2 and, since it comes chronologically earlier, actually foreshadows it. What I refer to here is a passage already mentioned a few chapters ago: Luke 4.

This earlier episode in the Luke-Acts narrative is rich with meaning for believers today. Here Jesus, the first Pentecostal, is front and center. The missional themes are clear. Good news, freedom, vision, favor—these are powerful, evocative, and Kingdom-centered realities close to the heart and mission of God.

It is worth considering the particular moment in Jesus' life in which this story takes place. Look just a little earlier in Luke 4, and there's something remarkable there. As early as verse 1, the Holy Spirit is at work. Jesus is described as both "full of the Holy Spirit" and as being "led by the Spirit." This, of course, is the introduction to his temptation in the wilderness. There, guided and empowered by God's own Spirit, Jesus resists the devil. In verse 13, the devil leaves Jesus.

By verse 14, Jesus returns to Galilee. Luke specifically says that He is there "in the power of the Spirit." I realize it is a little chronologically suspect to do so, but I would go as far as to say that this is Jesus at His most Pentecostal. The Holy Spirit is deeply at work in and through Him here in terms of presence, guidance, and power. It is an important moment in Luke's narrative for a reason, and ought to be a foundational place for us to understand more about what God is all about.

It is in this very Spirit-infused moment that Jesus reads and restates the words of Isaiah 61. I have already discussed how I believe these statements to be powerful announcements of the Kingdom of God. Understanding them here in the power of the Spirit only amplifies this reality. Good news, Jesus says, to the poor. Freedom for prisoners. New sight for the blind in our midst. Release from oppression.

In the scene in the synagogue, Jesus concludes his reading by proclaiming together with Isaiah "the year of the Lord's favor." Then, in what my mind imagines to be a scene worthy of a Hollywood movie, Jesus rolls up the scroll and sits down. His reading is complete. His announcement is over. The pages of the spiritual calendar have turned and the Lord's favor is upon the people in a new year that is much longer than a single set of 365 days. It is a new season, a new era. It is the mission of God the Father, proclaimed here in the words and actions of the Spirit-empowered Son.

A PENTECOSTAL MISSION, A MISSION IN THE SPIRIT

The mission that Jesus outlines here is deeply Pentecostal, even if the Day of Pentecost is, at this point in history, still a few years off. However, it is also deeply missional. This Pentecostal missionality is powerful, inspiring, and wide-ranging, bringing together the physical and the spiritual in a balanced and forceful manner. It blows apart any assumption that these things belong in separate boxes, or that God only really cares about one and not the other.

Everything that happens after this in Jesus' ministry—and that He aims to do in us as the body of Christ—is stated plainly here. God is on a mission to break down the devil's earthly and spiritual strongholds, and he calls and empowers us to follow after him in this great work.

Over the years, Pentecostals have a track record of embracing this mission. Bearing witness to God in word and deed. Caring for soul and body. Loving our neighbors as Christ loved us. Being ready to share our faith at a moment's notice. Listening to the Spirit's leading in ways both ordinary and extraordinary. Responding to the world's brokenness by offering the message of spiritual salvation and meeting the needs of those bound by earthly oppression, sickness, poverty, disaster—you name it. This is the mission of God.

As I ponder this, I cannot help but think of an organization called Convoy of Hope, which is a relief agency closely tied to the Pentecostal fellowship known as the Assemblies of God. As their website notes: "Convoy of Hope was founded in 1994 by the Donaldson family. Their inspiration for starting the organization can be traced back to the many people who helped their family after their father, Harold, was killed by a drunk driver in 1969. Today, more than 80 million people have been served throughout the world by Convoy of Hope. We are proud that we work through churches, businesses, government agencies and other nonprofits to provide help and hope to those who are impoverished, hungry and hurting."

The Spirit-led leadership of Convoy of Hope embraces their evangelistic calling even as they commit themselves to serving the physical needs of others. Truly they are living as missional Pentecostals.[21]

A CONCLUDING POSTSCRIPT

My sincere hope is that in this chapter I have made a convincing case that the Pentecostal call and the missional call are merely two sides of the same coin. To do this, I have focused especially on Luke

4. It is there—as elsewhere—we can clearly see Jesus as the first Pentecostal.

And now, another moment of confession: Luke 4 is—as I mentioned earlier—one of those Bible passages that holds particular meaning for me. It is, in no small way, how I found myself doing what I am now doing. God used a person preaching this very passage to call me—quite directly—to Himself. He used it to show me what the Pentecostal life was all about.

When I was a younger man, there was a time I was convinced that the life of ministry was not really for me. I was going to be an academic, I thought, and that was all there was to it. I was also a student at a Presbyterian seminary, and over the course of my first year of study, their more ordered and intellectual style began to entice me away from what I perceived to be a less than ideal Pentecostal background. I had grown up in the Assemblies of God, but in the few years preceding my early adulthood it hadn't really felt like home. Whatever I had experienced through the Holy Spirit years before seemed increasingly distant, and all I had in front of me was a failing local congregation and a growing distaste for what I would have termed "Pentecostal weirdness."

In that season, God led me to a conference of Pentecostal seminary students from around the country. During the sessions and conversations that surrounded the meeting, I slowly began to realize that the experiences of my youth were neither bankrupt nor suspect. Far from it. Rather, the Pentecostal understanding of Christianity had power and truth behind it. There were deep thinkers there but, even more importantly, these same people were deeply connected with the wellsprings of God's Spirit.

God was working on my heart during those two summer weeks. He led me to a place where I began to understand my relationship with His Church in a new way. Part of this I have already described. Some of it, though, took place in a single evening.

One night during the conference I ended up attending a missions service. It was not an event directly connected to the program I was a part of, but I went anyway. On the face of it, the service was not anything special. But for me, it most definitely was. It was that night in 2003 that I was called to ministry in a definitive way.

I knew after leaving that service that ministry is what God had for me. The Lord spoke to me that night—in what can authentically be called a Pentecostal moment—and told me that serving His Church was a part of the mission He was giving me. Everything was different after that. I started the process of applying for ministerial credentials. I began volunteering at my local church. I ended up, a scant two years later, becoming a youth minister. I later spent six years training future ministers. And God's work continues on.

The service that night featured a message that focused, very specifically, on what Pentecostalism was all about. Through it and in the midst of it, God called me to ministry. The passage that the sermon was based upon? Luke 4, of course. I daresay its theme has personally impacted me more than any other single portion of Scripture. Through that night, that preacher, and that message, God impressed me into His mission and helped set the course for my life.

Following Jesus means following Jesus the Pentecostal. True missionality embraces the Spirit's mission and should be empowered by it. Rather than shy from Pentecost, therefore, missionally-minded believers (which should, dare I say, be all of us) should seek it more. By the same measure, Pentecostal experience is and must always be missionally centered and focused. Why? Because Jesus is.

Pentecost—rightly understood, experienced, and appreciated—enables and deepens the potential for transformative mission. I will be so bold as to say this, and with it I will close: a Pentecostal who claims to embrace the Spirit in ways that have nothing to do with the outward-focused mission of God in Acts 2 and Luke 4 is not a true Pentecostal.

What does it mean for these two things to come together in a practical, hands-on way? What does it mean for Pentecostals to follow Jesus, the first Pentecostal? To help answer these questions, we invite you to consider some of the principles and suggestions Don and I will lay out in the next chapters.

CHAPTER EIGHT

PRACTICAL THEOLOGY FOR MISSIONAL PENTECOSTALS

ONE OF THE REASONS we wrote this book is to provide a deeper missional focus. We are surrounded by six million people in the Pacific Northwest who regard the teachings of Jesus as helpful, at best, and the Christian Church as irrelevant to their lives. It is into this region that God has thrust our ministers and churches with the mission to "bring the hope of Jesus to our communities."

We cannot reach these people with the gospel in our own strength or with clever ideas, strategies, and systems. Although these are incredibly helpful, we need more. We need the power of the Holy Spirit in our own lives as followers of Jesus, in our leaders, and in our churches.

We are not saying the Holy Spirit is not at work in ministers and churches now. He is. He has been at work on our planet since creation, but the day of Pentecost introduced a new endowment of power into the lives of those who follow Jesus. Something spectacular happened to the Church on that day, which leads us to conclude that we are capable of much greater spiritual influence in our region, culture, and society.

As a student of the Bible, you know it was, and is, God's plan to save the world by sending Christ to die on the cross. He paid our ransom, and while this is not the place for a long discourse on soteriology, that is the reason for Christ's birth, death, resurrection, and ascension.

Satan sought to kill Jesus at his birth and several times during his ministry, but to no avail. His purpose in trying to kill Jesus was that death was Satan's arena. No one had ever escaped from death, and if Satan could bring about Jesus' death, the mission of the Savior would be over, with mankind remaining in Satan's control.

As a student of the Bible, you also know that Christ was opposed by the "god of this world," our archenemy Satan. The mission and ministry of Jesus was a direct battle with the prince of this world. Jesus prophesied this conflict would take place, and Satan would be defeated.

> "Now judgment is upon this world; now the ruler of this world will be cast out." John 12:31

Later in the New Testament, the apostle John tells us this is the very purpose for which Jesus appeared: to destroy the works of the devil.

> "The one who practices sin is of the devil; for the devil has sinned from the beginning. The Son of God appeared for this purpose, to destroy the works of the devil." 1 John 3:8

The battle rages between Satan and Jesus during his earthly ministry. We see episodes of this spiritual warfare in the gospels, as Jesus contends with the enemy directly while fasting in the desert (Luke 4:1-13). He also faces the temptation from Satan in the Garden of Gethsemane to turn away from the cross (Matt. 26:36-46). For Jesus, the warfare for our salvation is constant, real, and personal.

When Jesus hangs on the cross, with the sin of the world imputed upon him, and he finally dies, Satan actually believes he has won. He could not believe that the Son of God would condescend to become a man and enter his domain. Satan believes he has defeated the

Godhead by breaking it up through death. The contest that started in heaven when he was cast out is finally over, and he has won... or so he believes.

TWO CRUSHING EVENTS TO SATAN'S KINGDOM

Two events happened on Earth over the next two months that bring holy shock and awe to Satan's world, as the Father unveils the next phases of his plan. The first event is the resurrection of Jesus.

Holy Scripture, as well as historical evidence, tells us Jesus rose from the dead, having conquered death, hell, and the grave. This had never happened before. Yes, people had died and been raised from the dead before, but no one had ever been raised from death before. Jesus conquered death! This shook Satan to the core.

Everyone who had been raised from the dead in the Old Testament and the New Testament would eventually taste death. They only had their temporary existence on Earth extended for a while. They would each die again in due course. When Jesus was raised from the dead, however, he was raised from death, and he would never taste death again. Because we are "in Christ," we, too, will be resurrected from death.

> "Now God has not only raised the Lord, but will also raise us up through His power." 1 Corinthians 6:14

> "Knowing that He who raised the Lord Jesus will raise us also with Jesus and will present us with you." 1 Corinthians 4:14

Death is the last enemy to be destroyed (I Cor. 15:26), and Jesus is the firstfruits of all who will be rescued from death. This means death is no longer Satan's domain. He has lost his control of the region he had dominated since the Garden of Eden.

This is what was revealed to the apostle Paul, as he brought correction to the Corinthian Church, who was being told the resurrection had already taken place.

> "When the perishable has been clothed with the imperishable, and the mortal with immortality, then the saying that is written will come true: 'Death has been swallowed up in victory.

> "'Where, O death, is your victory? Where, O death, is your sting?'

> "The sting of death is sin, and the power of sin is the law. But thanks be to God! He gives us the victory through our Lord Jesus Christ." 1 Corinthians 15:54-56

Death used to have victory; now it no longer does. Death had a sting because of sin; now we are free. Death was swallowed up in Christ's victory. When we are raised with Christ in resurrection, we are not just raised from the dead; we are free from death!

When the resurrection happened, it sent shock waves through the satanic ranks, but that is just the first act. The follow up to Jesus' resurrection and forty days of ministry is the outpouring of the Holy Spirit, and I want to suggest to you that this single event has an even greater debilitating effect on Satan's camp than the resurrection of Jesus.

The day of Pentecost is the second shockwave to Satan. Think about this for a moment. Satan has just endured the fight of his existence. The Son of God, who has rescued mankind and destroyed Satan's power on Earth, has just beat Satan. Satan has held mankind in his grip since the Garden of Eden, and now that hold is gone. He is defeated.

He barely recovers from this episode, when the Father sends his gift, the Holy Spirit, to fill all the believers who heed Jesus' command to wait for this gift. This outpouring of the Holy Spirit brings a level of spiritual power, unknown up to this point, to these followers of Jesus. The Scripture below tells us how the day of Pentecost got started.

> "When the day of Pentecost came, they were all together in one place. Suddenly a sound like the blowing of a violent wind came from heaven and filled the whole house where they were sitting. They saw what seemed to be tongues of fire that separated and came to rest on each of them. All of them were filled with the Holy Spirit and began to speak in other tongues as the Spirit enabled them." Acts 2:1-4

This is how the day of Pentecost began, but that is not how the day ends. Peter preaches boldly, starting with the prophecy of Joel, giving a full account of Jesus' life, and ending by accusing the crowd of killing Jesus, who God raised from the dead.

They are so taken by the power of his words and impact of the Holy Spirit's work in this moment that they scream out, "What shall we do?" Peter and the other apostles tell them to repent and be baptized.

> "Peter replied, 'Repent and be baptized, every one of you, in the name of Jesus Christ for the forgiveness of your sins. And you will receive the gift of the Holy Spirit. The promise is for you and your children and for all who are far off—for all whom the Lord our God will call.'" Acts 2:38-39

Peter tells them that by following repentance and baptism, they will receive the gift of the Holy Spirit. This promise is for generations and for all whom God calls.

The verses below tell us how the day of Pentecost ends, with three thousand coming to faith in Christ. The pattern of people daily worshiping, meeting in homes, and coming to Christ is started.

> "Every day they continued to meet together in the temple courts. They broke bread in their homes and ate together with glad and sincere hearts, praising God and enjoying the favor of all the people. And the Lord added to their number daily those who were being saved." Acts 2:46-47

This shockwave hits Satan's kingdom. Up to this point, he has had to contend with the Son of God and a few dedicated followers, but that is no longer the case. For the first time in history, all the followers of Jesus are filled with the same Spirit that fills Jesus. Paul the apostle later confirms this:

> "…and who through the Spirit of holiness was appointed the Son of God in power by his resurrection from the dead: Jesus Christ our Lord." Romans 1:4

> "And if the Spirit of him who raised Jesus from the dead is living in you, he who raised Christ from the dead will also give life to your mortal bodies because of his Spirit who lives in you." Romans. 8:11

On the day of Pentecost, what shakes Satan is that he went from contending with one Spirit-filled God follower named Jesus, to 120 Spirit-filled believers, who all have the same power to overcome. Within a day, those numbers increase even more.

Now all believers have the same power in them that Jesus has in himself. Every believer can now take authority over Satan, just as Jesus has. Every believer can proclaim this good news, and every believer can help new believers receive the same power, just like Jesus.

From Satan's point of view, he cannot keep up with the growth of the church or with new believers being filled with the Holy Spirit. The growth continues through the book of Acts, with thousands of new believers coming to faith in Christ and being filled with the Holy Spirit. Satan may have thought he had won at the cross, but he lost, and he lost in a huge way.

As a young minister, I had a dream or a vision. I am really not sure which, but it was vivid. It remains with me to this day, and that experience touches on this topic.

In my dream, I saw Satan standing with the Earth in one hand. It was entirely dark, and he was snarling and smiling in a satisfying way as if to say, "I'm in control. I own you. You're entirely mine."

At that moment, one light appeared. In my dream, I clearly understood that this was the light of the gospel. It was small and seemed insignificant. It was obvious, though, that Satan hated this light and wanted to destroy it. In an instant, he lifted a huge club and smashed the Earth where the light was, and it went out. He then smiled a satisfying smile, as if to say, "I'm in control again, and the kingdom of darkness reigns again."

Then in a moment, two lights appear where the one had been smashed. Satan hit these lights and put them out, and again smiled that smug and satisfying smile. Again, the world was dark, and he believed he was in control.

Then four lights appeared, and he smashed them. Then eight lights appeared, and he smashed them. Every time he smashed the lights on the Earth, they came back two-fold. He could not stop himself, though. Even when he knew that his attacks on the Earth doubled the number of lights, he still kept hitting until the entire planet was covered in the light of the gospel. Then the dream ended.

At the day of Pentecost, believers were given the same Spirit as

Jesus in order to spread the gospel. In fact, the book of Acts calls the Holy Spirit, the Spirit of Jesus (Acts 16:7). On the day of Pentecost, Satan thought he was fully defeated, because he had gone from dealing with one person filled with the Spirit (Jesus), to 120 people filled with the same Spirit, to possibly thousands filled with the same Spirit. It is impossible for him to keep up with the multiplication of the gospel.

Persecution does not stop the gospel; it only spreads it further around the Earth. Eventually, the gospel of Jesus conquers the Roman Empire, and missionaries are sent everywhere in the known world. It is not until the Dark Ages, when God's Word is banned from his people, that Satan begins to get an increasing foothold. This foothold remains until the Reformation is launched in 1517, eventually putting the Scriptures back into the hands of the people.

As we will see in the next chapter, God's work is never contained or restrained. As his servants, we are to realize we are filled with his Spirit for the purpose of spreading the gospel.

Therefore, if we are filled with the Holy Spirit and called by God to share our faith, and if we as leaders are to help others do the same, what does this mean to a local church or mission work?

CHAPTER NINE
HOW WE GOT HERE

GOD'S WORK IS NEVER CONTAINED or restrained; God's will is going to be accomplished. He is always at work in the world, and as his servants, we are filled with his Spirit in order to spread the gospel. That is our missional priority, and it is to be realized on a daily basis—not just on Sundays.

At the beginning of this book, Josh and I both stated we have observed churches that focus on the mission of the gospel. Even though they are Pentecostal churches, they often have difficulty knowing where and how to fit in the ministry of the Holy Spirit. Our former model of the voice gifts of tongues, interpretation of tongues, and prophecy being used in a Sunday morning service no longer seems to fit with our current worship culture, at least not like it has in churches in past decades.

Pentecostal churches that have focused on the voice gifts being regularly exercised in a Sunday service often seem to have a difficult time seeing people come to Christ. They pray for the lost, and occasionally people come to faith in Christ. Unfortunately, it is not to the degree that they would like to see.

Many people have a tendency to gravitate towards tradition, and for the most part, nothing is wrong with that, until the tradition gets in the way of mission. The Holy Spirit is doing something new all the time, and Scripture tells us we are to take note of what is new and keep in step with the Spirit.

"See, I am doing a new thing! Now it springs up; do you not perceive it? I am making a way in the wilderness and streams in the wasteland." Isaiah 43:19

"Since we live by the Spirit, let us keep in step with the Spirit." Galatians 5:25

From a spiritual perspective, we are living in a wasteland. Experiencing something new from the Holy Spirit making a way in our own wilderness would be a welcome and refreshing change.

I want to be clear here: what we are sharing is an idea. We are on a journey of exploration, and we are inviting you to join us. We are not saying we are more in touch with the Holy Spirit and are here to proclaim a new way. On the other hand, we are saying we have observed what many others have also observed, and the Holy Spirit wants his power to flow through us beyond our Sunday morning experience. We have to consider how this could happen if we are to be effective in our missional assignment to "make disciples" as Jesus commanded.

Maybe the Holy Spirit is doing something new, and we are watching it unfold before our eyes as we take a long look.

Consider our history over the last one hundred years. As a Pentecostal fellowship, we have seen some amazing changes. Our fellowship started as a group of ecclesiastical misfits who had been filled with the Holy Spirit and called to ministry. We were pastors and leaders from various faith traditions who had been impacted by the outpouring of the Holy Spirit in the early 1900s, and we had to respond.

We found support and encouragement from being together, and from these connections, our Assemblies of God fellowship was born. Out of that first gathering in 1914, while the world was at war, we made a commitment that would sink deeply into our DNA as a movement. That pledge was, "We commit ourselves to the greatest evangelism the world has ever seen."

We began to send missionaries around the world and plant churches. Our focus was on reaching lost people, and we felt propelled by the Holy Spirit to this task. Since the Holy Spirit energized us, we also shared the teaching on being baptized in the Holy Spirit. For us historically, the two subjects of salvation and the baptism in the Holy Spirit were in tandem, just like the apostles believed in the book of Acts.

This continued for the next few decades, and following World War II, almost every denomination experienced growth through the 1940s and 1950s. We not only had a "baby boom" in our population, we had a "Bible boom," as we saw churches flourish in our nation. We experienced some years of persecution as Pentecostals, but largely, we enjoyed this growth chapter in our history.

While we rushed into the 1960s and 1970s, we saw some turbulent times socially, as political unrest surfaced surrounding the war in Vietnam. We saw our president resign, the first ever in our history. We also saw the "Jesus People" movement rise with thousands coming to Christ, and Dave Wilkerson launched Teen Challenge. This era featured healing campaigns with noted evangelists. During these two decades, Pentecostal churches began to grow significantly.

Our own church in Seattle opened its arms to young people with long hair and jeans. It was common for a twenty-something in jeans to be standing next to a fifty-something in a suit and tie. It was an amazing time as stories flooded our churches of people being delivered from gangs and drugs and finding Jesus.

Then came the 1970s and 1980s, and what we have come to call the Charismatic Renewal. During this time in our history, three remarkable changes took place.

1. Mainline Churches Receive the Holy Spirit

First, many people in traditionally mainline churches began to find the baptism in the Holy Spirit. They found a spiritual refreshing they had never known before and were deeply changed. Businessmen banded together and formed the Full Gospel Business Men's Association, and conferences arose. Women's Aglow was formed, and they had their own conferences. Churches began to fill.

Merely attending a charismatic conference once a year, though, was not enough. These folks wanted to see the power of the Holy Spirit in their own churches, and conflicts began to surface. Mainline churches were not about to change their doctrinal positions, so people simply left their church homes and flooded into Pentecostal churches, many of them to our fellowship.

During this season, we reached new heights, and churches of thousands in attendance broke on the scene. Huge buildings began to spring up, and the term "megachurch" was coined. It was all very exciting, and the future looked bright. It seemed no end was in sight to this increase of people in our services.

This growth continued until mainline churches began to be open to the moving of the Spirit and, in fact, changed their doctrine to accommodate what was happening. We saw the rise of charismatic Catholic churches, Presbyterian churches, Methodist churches, and even Baptist churches open to the Holy Spirit. Growth slowed down, as the previous flood from mainline churches was greatly reduced. The 1980s saw the wind of the Spirit blow across denominational lines, and we rejoiced in how the Holy Spirit was moving.

2. Churches Lose Their Outward Focus

Secondly, churches during this era began to lose their outward focus. We had seen amazing transfer growth for the last two decades, yet we actually set aside our outward focus. This loss of an outward focus was both subtle and incremental, and it took place during the same period. The three ministries in most churches that began to decline during this season included Sunday night services, Sunday school, and altar calls.

Historically through the early 1970s, almost all of our churches held a Sunday night service, and these services tended to be more evangelistic. Sunday night services had not started until the 1700s when whale oil became available for lighting. Churches were one of the only organizations that could afford this luxury lighting, so the evening service began. They were called a vesper service (Latin for "evening"), but for the first seventeen centuries, the church held no regular evening service.

We also had thriving Sunday schools, which were birthed historically out of an evangelistic endeavor. Robert Raikes, an Anglican layman burdened for the children who worked six days a week but could not read or write, founded Sunday school in England in the late 1700s. Their only day off was Sunday, and most of them had access to a Bible, so he started Sunday school for these children. Although Raikes died in 1811, by 1831, over a million children were enrolled. Within a short time, this movement arrived in America and was adopted into local churches. For many years, Sunday schools were a significant outreach tool. (In fact, our own church in Seattle was founded in 1938 as an outreach Sunday school.) Again, for seventeen centuries, though, the church had no Sunday school.

Finally, nearly every service was traditionally closed with an "altar call," in which people would come forward to receive Christ or pray. The altar call had its roots in the "brush arbor" services of the Wesleys, the "anxious bench" of Charles Finney, and the mass evangelism of Dwight Moody and later Billy Graham. The Wesleys were driven out of their Anglican tradition, both for Charles' songwriting (he used secular music and added Christian lyrics) and John's preaching. Their only choice was to meet out in the open, which was called a "brush arbor" service, and eventually became known as a camp meeting service. All of these evangelists closed their meetings effectively with an altar call, asking people to come forward to receive Christ. For 1800 years, however, the church had no such altar calls.

What I want us to see is that the Sunday night service, Sunday school, and altar calls were used by the Sprit in a mighty way and for a season. Is it possible the Holy Spirit wants to do something new again, in our day?

During these decades of the 1970s and 1980s, Sunday night services began to be discontinued. Small groups replaced Sunday school, and regular altar calls were greatly diminished, if not stopped altogether in local churches.

These decisions were not necessarily poor decisions, and they were often based on meeting needs more effectively or simply responding to the obvious. Sunday night services were often considered a repeat of Sunday morning, and as multiple services became more popular, it made sense not to wear out volunteers with a Sunday night service, especially with diminishing evening crowds.

Small groups replaced Sunday school, partly because multiple services provided no space for this ministry and because a decentralized ministry was preferable. Having people meet in homes instead of a classroom was more relational and more easily replicated, at little or no expense to the church. It also developed more leaders in the church.

Altar calls were coming to be understood as an ineffective ministry tool. Why would we ask someone new to our church, to receive Christ only by walking up to the "altar" in front of a room full of strangers? It was seen as being insensitive, so having someone respond with a raised hand or on a response card became the norm. The place for them to make their faith public was through water baptism, rather than the altar call. This made sense to many leaders both from a practical and biblical point of view.

The value of these three—a focused evangelistic service Sunday night, an expected altar call in each service, and a thriving Sunday school—was that these elements helped the local church remain outward focused because it was built into the culture and practice of the local church. The church remained outward focused by an entrenched system.

As these three areas began to evaporate, and because of both the American and local church cultures shifting, many churches lost their outward focus. Reaching lost people was no longer a priority, and we began to see our church growth slow overall and then wane.

I am not saying we should return to the days of Sunday night service, or Sunday school, or even altar calls, although a public response from time to time can be important. As I said, the Christian church thrived for 1800 years without Sunday school, evening services, or altar calls. Nevertheless, it is evident that churches cannot survive without a focus on reaching lost people with the gospel of Jesus!

The loss of these three entrenched areas of ministry in the local church created a void in missional focus that allowed the third change, which is directly connected to the power of the Holy Spirit in the life of believers and the local church.

3. The Gifts of the Spirit Become Inward Focused

As stated at the beginning of this chapter, when our fellowship was born, outreach was in our DNA. We sent missionaries around the world and planted churches, all empowered by the Holy Spirit. The Spirit's power was present to help us focus on the mission of Jesus, but over time, that focus waned.

As I studied the history of my own church in Seattle, which I attended in the 1970s and pastored for twenty years starting in 1995, I saw our outreach focus fade. Our history in the 1970s and 1980s showed us trending away from being outreach focused and becoming a center for the charismatic revival, where people attended largely for the blessing received during a service.

The church grew dramatically during this time, but not primarily from new converts. The growth came from people leaving other non-charismatic churches to attend ours. This was typical of many churches in our fellowship. In this season of our fellowship's history, the gifts of the Spirit were modeled for us in operation, almost exclusively during the context of a Sunday morning service.

Believers were not trained as much by their pastors to hear the still, small voice of the Spirit during the week or to recognize a word of wisdom or a word of knowledge. We were not trained to pray for healing for lost people at our job. Our experience with the power of the Spirit was usually limited to a ninety-minute session on Sunday morning at our local church, which we called "the service."

This in itself is interesting, because the term "service" was developed nearly two centuries ago when church members gathered on Sunday. As a part of their worship experience, their pastor would assign where they were to "serve" in their community the next week. Churches existed to bless and help their communities. From that time, the term evolved into church service, meaning a worship gathering for us, and not a "service" that would focus on helping the community.

As a result of the lack of emphasis on reaching lost people and the demise of our own internal church systems that kept us focused on reaching the lost, church services began to be increasingly more about ourselves. Pastors and church leaders asked, "What does our church need?" not "How can our church serve our community?"

We began to hear phrases like, "What did you get out of that service?" or "I'm not really being fed." Such statements reveal the focus is not about the mission of reaching lost people, but about the personal benefit received from attending church. We became ecclesiastical consumers, rather than an army of compassion.

Simultaneously, we focused on the gifts of the Spirit for our own benefit and our own emotions. It was a good service when we had a message in tongues, and a lesser service when that did not happen. It was not about being trained and equipped for ministry during the week. It was primarily about how church made us "feel." Many churches devolved into Christian clubs, rather than focused causes for the gospel.

Jesus teaches us that those he has given as gifts to the church lead the church, and their main job is to equip us for service.

> "So Christ himself gave the apostles, the prophets, the evangelists, the pastors and teachers, to equip his people for works of service." Ephesians 4:11-12

The actual reason we gather on Sundays is not to make us feel good, although that may very well happen. The reason we gather is to become equipped to move the mission of Jesus forward in our corner of the world on a daily basis.

Everything we have received from Jesus is to help in that holy and righteous endeavor. Jesus sent us the Holy Spirit not to make us feel good, but to be empowered to reach the lost. The Holy Spirit has given us his gifts not to make us feel good, but to minister to others, especially those outside of a personal experience of God's love.

I think over time, we began to seek the gifts of the Spirit and even to use the gifts for our own benefit. By this I mean we wanted to experience the gifts for the emotional boost they provided. This was an unintentional shift, but it happened nonetheless.

We became Spirit-filled Christians ninety minutes a week in a service for our benefit, as opposed to being Spirit-filled all week long and seeing ourselves as local missionaries to our community. It is interesting that churches that try to contain the gifts of the Spirit exclusively to a worship service tend towards the extreme, but churches that teach their people to allow the gifts in their lives in the marketplace on a daily basis avoid such extremes.

I have a personal theory regarding why we see fewer utterances in tongues and fewer prophecies in our local church services and in fewer churches than we did several decades ago. I think God is cleaning us up for something great. Here is my story and theory.

As a boy, I grew up in Eastern Washington going to Silver Lake Bible Camp. Each year for a week, my parents would take me to camp, where we enjoyed games, music, and great services. As I said in the beginning of this book, I experienced the baptism in the Holy Spirit at youth camp. One of the great joys of camp, for me, was to get up early and fish off the dock for trout, which I was allowed to keep.

One year I caught a whopper. I was only about ten years old, and I could not wait to show my dad. This fish was bigger than any I had ever caught, and I remember racing towards the camp kitchen where he was helping prepare breakfast.

I yelled, "Dad, look at this!" I wanted him to be so proud of me and what I had accomplished. He came out from behind the counter and looked at my fish with a big smile. I knew he was proud of me, but his smile told me he had more to say.

He said, "Don, that's a big fish alright, bigger than anything you've ever caught before, but this fish looks different than other fish you've caught, doesn't it?"

I had to admit that it was different, so I agreed with him. "Yes, Dad, it is different. What is it?"

He smiled and said, "Don, you've caught a carp. You don't want to eat that fish, and I don't want to cook it. The best thing you can do is throw it back in the lake. I'm sorry, son. It is a big fish, and I'm proud of you for catching it, but it's actually fish we don't want. Go throw it back, and let's have breakfast."

The next year at camp, I could not wait to go fishing again, but I wanted to avoid catching another carp if I could. As I ran down to the lake with my fishing rod, one of the camp leaders stopped me.

He said, "I'm sorry. There is no fishing this year—there's no fish to be caught. The lake has been cleansed and all the fish removed. There were too many suckers, and they were killing the trout. Next year, they will be planting good fish, but for now, the lake is empty."

I could not believe it, so I asked him, "Last year I caught a carp. My dad said it was not a good fish. Is that also called a sucker?" He smiled, nodded, and said, "Yes, that's right. Be patient, and next year you'll catch some good fish." He was right. To this day, that is the only carp I have ever caught.

As I reflect on that story from my childhood, I wonder if the Holy Spirit is doing something similar. I wonder if he is cleansing the church, retraining us, and teaching us that the gifts of the Spirit are to be used primarily for the mission and not our own excitement. We are called to bring the Spirit's power to the marketplace and to our neighborhood, not just to a worship gathering.

As we look at the book of Acts, we notice that the Spirit's power was released in homes, on the street, and in the marketplace much more than at a worship service. This stands in stark contrast to what many churches experience, where their only contact during the week with the Holy Spirit's power is in a worship service.

If we use Acts as a model for the church, we have to conclude that training our people to allow God to use them daily is part of that early church model. Training them to allow the gifts to flow through them daily is more in line than relegating the Spirit's work in a faith community to Sunday only. Consider these power encounters as written in the Scriptures.

In Acts, two people are raised from the dead—one by Peter and one by Paul (Acts 9:36-42, 20:9-12). Peter's miracle happens in a home and Paul's in an upper room during a teaching time.

Acts lists a series of miraculous healings and exorcisms. Peter heals a lame man at the temple gate (3:1-16). Ananias prays for Saul and sees him healed (9:17-18). Peter heals the paralytic Aeneas (9:33-35), and Paul cures a lame man in Lystra (14:7-9). Paul is stoned and then miraculously healed in Lystra (14:19). Paul casts a demon out of a girl (16:16-18), and Paul heals Publius's father from a fever and dysentery (28:7-8).

All of these power encounters happen outside a worship service.

The power of the Holy Spirit is manifested in public. The Holy Spirit also displays power in miraculous afflictions, even punishment.

Ananias and Sapphira are struck down for lying (5:5-11), and Paul is blinded on the road to Damascus (9:8-9). Herod is slain by an angel (12:23), and Paul temporarily blinds the sorcerer Elymas (13:9-12). Although we may be uncomfortable with this part of his work, it did indeed happen.

The Holy Spirit's power is injected into nature in a way that demands recognition. He brings a violent wind into the upper room (2:2-6). The building in Jerusalem shakes following the apostles' prayer for boldness (4:31), and all the apostles in prison are released together after an angel opens the prison doors (5:17-25). Philip is snatched up by the Holy Spirit and transported to Azotus (8:39), and Peter is liberated a second time from prison by an angel (12:5-11). Chains fall off Paul and Silas in prison (16:25-30), and Paul shakes off a poisonous viper from his arm after being bitten (28:3-6).

From a collective point of view, the power of the Holy Spirit is displayed publicly in a variety of ways in Acts. The apostles perform signs and wonders (2:43 and 5:12), and Peter's shadow cures the sick in the street (5:15). Crowds from towns outside Jerusalem are healed (5:16), and Stephen performs great signs and wonders (6:8). Philip heals the lame and casts out demons in Samaria (8:6-8, 13). Paul and Barnabas perform miracles on their missionary journey (14:3), and they perform signs and wonders among the Gentiles (15:12). Healing and deliverance through handkerchiefs and aprons occur after Paul touches them (19:11-12), and Paul heals all the sick on Malta (28:9).

What if those of us who follow Jesus were always ready to minister in the power of the Spirit anywhere, like the apostles did? What would happen if we prayed for our neighbors over the backyard fence and saw people healed in the grocery store following prayer?

One day, I was working in my yard shoveling dirt. Brenda and I were helping with a church plant at the time, and we had two small daughters. We had gotten to know our neighbors, Mike and Pam, and even hosted them for dinner. They learned we were pastors, and we learned they knew nothing about church. Apparently, they had no interest in knowing more.

Mike was quite sick and had been home for several days from his job at an oil refinery. As I continued working in my yard, I was prompted by the Holy Spirit to go and pray for Mike at his house. I knew I was to do this, but I resisted for about an hour while I worked. I kept thinking this prompting would leave me, but it did not.

I had prayed for many people who were sick and had seen some wonderful healings, but they were all in the context of a Sunday worship service. Church was my turf. To go into my neighbor's home, a neighbor I barely knew, and ask if I could pray for him was a stretch for me, but the Holy Spirit would not relent.

I continued to resist praying for Mike. The reason I resisted praying for Mike was not just that he was not a follower of Jesus, did not go to church, read the Bible, or pray.

The reason I resisted was that the Holy Spirit made it quite clear that I was to pray for Mike in his home and to verbally command the sickness to leave his body. I was not to pray a nice, peaceful prayer of blessing, sprinkling clergy dust with my words, and then leave. I was to be bold, albeit not offensive, commanding the sickness in Jesus' name to leave Mike's body at once.

After wrestling with the Spirit for an hour, I was now willing to pray for him outside of church and go into his home. I put down my shovel and walked over to Mike's house. He was so sick that he just called from the couch, and I went in.

He said, "Hi, Don. I can't get up. I've been on the couch for days. I can't get over this."

"I know you're sick," I replied, "That's why I'm here. I've been feeling like I was supposed to come over and pray for you to get well."

Mike just looked at me. That was not what he had anticipated. As he waited expectantly, I proceeded.

"Mike, I'm supposed to pray for you in a very direct way so that Jesus will bring healing into your body. I would like to put my hands on you and talk directly to your sickness, commanding it to leave in Jesus' name. Is it ok with you if I pray this way?"

He certainly did not know how to respond. What could he say, and what did he have to lose? He simply nodded and answered, "If you think it will help, I'm up for anything."

I moved across the room, laid hands on him, and commanded the sickness to leave his body in Jesus' name. I did not yell, but I was very direct in my prayer, speaking to the sickness. The whole episode took about ninety seconds, and then I went back to my house.

The next day when I saw Mike, he told me he slept all night for the first time in weeks and woke up well. He was on his way back to work. That short powerful encounter provided an opportunity to talk more with Mike in the weeks ahead, although we moved soon after that. I did not have the opportunity to lead Mike to Christ, but I am sure Jesus used this experience to move him forward.

Sometimes I dream and pray about what might happen if the people in our churches were filled with the Spirit to the point that we are ready at a moment's notice to respond to needs. What would happen if we were Pentecostal on the street, in the marketplace, and in our neighborhoods—not just on Sunday?

CHAPTER TEN

FINDING OUR WAY FORWARD

AS WE DRAW OUR DISCUSSION TO A CLOSE, I would like to conclude with some final thoughts for us to consider that may help us find our way forward.

ACTS AS A MODEL

We hold all Scripture sacred and fully believe that God has given us the Bible, as Paul trained young Timothy in the verses below.

> "All Scripture is God-breathed and is useful for teaching, rebuking, correcting and training in righteousness, so that the servant of God may be thoroughly equipped for every good work." 2 Timothy 3:16-17

I was raised with a thorough understanding of the Scriptures in the light of Pentecostal theology, with a clear focus on 1 Corinthians to support that theology. I believe clearly that 1 Corinthians needs to be in the mix, but we also need to understand that this entire book was written to solve a series of problems in the church.

Each chapter in 1 Corinthians identifies a problem in either behavior or theology that the apostle Paul addresses and corrects.

While this is helpful and needed, I believe that Acts is a better model for us than is 1 Corinthians.

Acts shows us the power of the gospel as it expands throughout the Roman empire and as the power of the Holy Spirit is manifested in the lives of ordinary people, who have now become dynamic leaders in this new movement.

It is also interesting that the power of the Spirit is mostly manifested in the daily lives of people and hardly ever in the context of a worship service. People are healed, demons cast out, and the gifts of the Spirit are seen in homes, on the street, and in the marketplace. This is in stark contrast to twenty-first century Pentecostals, who seem to largely experience the manifestation of the Holy Spirit's power in the context of a church service alone.

Additionally, as previously stated, the primary manifestations seen in many Pentecostal churches today have to do with the voice gifts of tongues, interpretation of tongues, and prophecy. While these gifts are clearly part of the Holy Spirit's work, we do not see them in operation in any of the worship services in the book of Acts.

Some churches in our own ministry network regularly have the voice gifts in operation as a part of their weekend worship experience, while other churches in our network do not. It would seem that both churches have a biblical foundation, with the later favoring the Acts model.

That being said, the power of the Spirit must be manifested in the lives of believers in the local church on a daily basis, which is the message we hope you are taking from this study. The simple fact is God uses his people to reach more people, and if we are not filled with the Spirit, in tune with the Spirit, and walking in the Spirit each day, we will not do our part to move the mission of Jesus forward.

Just as in the book of Acts, we need to be ordinary people, empowered by the Holy Spirit, doing extra ordinary tasks that draw people to the gospel.

MISSION FIRST, POWER SECOND

In my first place of ministry, my senior pastor and I used to play tennis together. He had taken some lessons from a professional tennis player, and he passed them on to me.

He advised, "Don, I was told by a tennis pro that there is a sequence of three parts to becoming a good tennis player. They are consistency, accuracy, and power. He told me many players want to show power first, but the power comes last. You have to first know where you are sending the ball before you add power."

He continued, "The bottom line is, if we show power in our swing, but almost always hit the ball into the net, what does it matter? You must first concentrate on consistently getting the ball over the net in the right direction, then add power."

At the time, I was a young man in ministry. He was trying to build my skills and to help me recognize the clear priority in these ministry skills. I think this story has some application for our study as well.

I have to confess that going into this study two years ago, I believed the mission of the gospel and the power of the Spirit were two sequential issues on equal footing. Much like accuracy and consistency in tennis could be seen as equal, we could see being missional and Pentecostal as equivalent. Nevertheless, they are not.

I have concluded that the mission of the gospel is first and must always be first. The following is why I believe this and why it is so important.

Jesus came first to introduce the mission of the gospel, and then the Father sent the Holy Spirit. Jesus' ministry was all about the mission of God, and Jesus clearly established the mission of reaching lost people. He also had the power of the Spirit working in his life as he healed the sick, cast out demons, and raised the dead, but Jesus' focus was always on the mission of God.

In addition to the parables of the lost coin, the lost sheep, and the lost son in Luke 15, two other Scriptures illustrate that the mission of reaching the lost was at the forefront of why Christ came. "For the Son of Man came to seek and to save the lost" (Luke 19:10). "The Son of Man did not come to be served, but to serve, and to give his life as a ransom for many" (Matt. 20:28). All of this was established long before the outpouring of the Holy Spirit.

Let me hasten to add that this is not an either/or proposition, meaning either we focus on the mission of the gospel, or we focus on the power of the Holy Spirit. That is part of the challenge that has produced directionless churches, resulting in being plateaued and even declining.

I am saying our focus as churches and church leaders must always be on the mission of the gospel, but we must be empowered by the Holy Spirit to do this mission. I believe this is exactly what Jesus said to us in his last words here on earth.

> "But you will receive power when the Holy Spirit comes on you; and you will be my witnesses in Jerusalem, and in all Judea and Samaria, and to the ends of the earth." Acts 1:8

If being filled with the Holy Spirit does not deepen the mission of the gospel to reach the lost and "be his witnesses," then we have missed what Jesus told us. If we believe being filled with the Holy Spirit is simply to draw us closer to God and to make us feel better in our faith or help us experience our faith at a deeper level, we are not following the Master's command.

Any teaching on the baptism of the Holy Spirit must be deeply connected to carrying the mission of the gospel forward.

Since the mission came first, followed by the power to fulfill the mission, the Holy Spirit will never do anything that would stop or hinder the mission he is empowering us to complete. Part of my concern is that simply having the voice gifts operate during a Sunday service can lull us into thinking we have the power of the Holy Spirit in our church, but our experience is restricted to activities inside the church building alone. The Holy Spirit is longing to use us outside the church during the week, in our neighborhoods, in our jobs, and in the marketplace.

Is anything happening in your church, being done in the name of the Holy Spirit, that actually impedes or slows the mission of the gospel? Are your people trained to recognize the inner prompting of the Holy Spirit to pray with someone, which could result in miraculous healing, or to offer some direction in a conversation, which is actually a word of knowledge or word of wisdom?

This is exactly what happened with Philip in Acts 8. As he proclaimed the good news of the kingdom, people were baptized, and miracles and signs were part of this mix. Even in this Scripture, the mission is mentioned first, then the power of the Spirit is manifested. Again, this is not an either/or proposition. We need to be mission focused and Spirit empowered.

PASTORS AS CULTURAL ARCHITECTS

Each church has a culture, and each pastor is the primary cultural architect of that local church. Paul presents this concept as he brings instruction to the Corinthian church.

> "By the grace God has given me, I laid a foundation as a wise builder, and someone else is building on it. But each one should build with care. For no one can lay any foundation other than the one already laid, which is Jesus Christ. If anyone builds on this foundation using gold, silver, costly stones, wood, hay or straw, their work will be shown for what it is, because the Day will bring it to light. It will be revealed with fire, and the fire will test the quality of each person's work. If what has been built

survives, the builder will receive a reward. If it is burned up, the builder will suffer loss but yet will be saved— even though only as one escaping through the flames." 1 Corinthians 3:10-15

Paul, speaking as an apostle, is declaring that he has laid the foundation by God's grace. He clearly tells us only one foundation— Jesus Christ—exists, but others are building on this foundation. In fact, many are building on this foundation. He then teaches that some are building with quality materials, and some are building with lesser quality. These builders will have their work tested by fire, and if it survives, they will receive a reward. If their work is burned up, they will be saved, but as one barely escaping.

Each of us is building our lives on the Rock—Christ Jesus—and how much more the church we are leading. The primary point in this Scripture is that many people are building in many different ways but each on the same foundation. This is the language of culture. Churches, each with a unique and different culture, are suited to their mission, location, and people, but the pastor is the primary architect of this culture.

Here is why this is important to our study: if the pastor is building a church culture with a missional foundation, but without the biblical teaching of the power of the Spirit, then it will be missionally focused but spiritually lethargic. The people will be focused on the mission but not empowered to fully accomplish it.

If the pastor is building a church through biblical teaching on the power of the Spirit, but without a focus on the mission of the gospel, then the people will be empowered but without direction. It is entirely possible the church then turns inward with more interest in "good services" than in reaching lost people.

This is why Paul wrote, "But each one should build with care" in verse 10, because much is riding on how we build. Pastor, you are the cultural architect of your church, and being both missional and Pentecostal matters.

TEACH PEOPLE ABOUT THE HOLY SPIRIT

How do you teach on the Holy Spirit? How do you teach about his gifts? How do you teach on the baptism of the Holy Spirit? How do you teach your people to fellowship with the Holy Spirit?

In September of 2017, about 1600 leaders from the Free Methodist, United Methodist, and other Wesleyan tradition churches were gathered in Franklin, Tennessee, for a conference. The conference theme was "Sowing for the Next Great Awakening."

The evening speaker was Sandy Millar, the pastor of Holy Trinity Brompton Church in London. This is without question the most influential church in Northern Europe.

Sandy's message was simple: we need the Holy Spirit in order to do what we have been called to do. He then went on to say being filled with the Holy Spirit is in the Bible, and it is for today.

He further stated, "I know most of you are afraid to yield to him, because you think it will make you weird, like something extreme you've seen on TV. You're concerned it will take you in emotional directions that will embarrass you."

At this point, Sandy knew he had the crowd's attention, and he was sensing he should continue leading them in this direction. God had something he wanted to do in this moment for this group of people.

Sandy continued, "While the Holy Spirit will direct you and empower you, he will not make you weird! Get that straight right now. So, I want you to sit back in your seats, refuse to be afraid, and start to speak in tongues. As you start, the Holy Spirit will join you. He will well up from within you, and a closer partnership will start to form than you've ever thought was possible. Are you ready? Begin."

Then this grandfatherly, white-haired man led everyone in the room into an experience with the Holy Spirit with glossolalia, and literally everyone in the room began speaking in tongues.

This story was relayed to me by one of our network pastors, Dr. Verlon Fosner. As Verlon was talking with me, he recalled, "My wife Melodee and I were stunned, then we were blessed, then we were stunned again. How could this have been so easy for a room full of concerned saints? I turned to the conference organizer, who I'm sure is a closet Pentecostal, and said, 'Am I really witnessing 1600 Methodists speaking in tongues?' To which he replied, 'Evidently.'"

I share this story with you, because in this setting, with clear teaching and calm, loving leadership, the Holy Spirit baptized hundreds of people. This was not an emotionally-driven event, but a simple invitation to experience the Holy Spirit in all his goodness.

Let me write out my confession here. Sometimes in ministry, we look back with joy, and other times we look back with measured regret. This is one of those times for me. I did not do a great job of teaching our people about the Holy Spirit. Especially after two years of intense study, I realize so much more could have been done. In fact, I resisted writing this book because I felt like such a poor example, but if my error can serve others, then I am duty-bound to share and continue to learn and grow.

Our church in Seattle was so charismatic and so extreme we needed to curb such prominence. In order to bring balance and establish a missional basis for ministry, we stopped all voice gifts from functioning in our Sunday services. It was difficult. Over the next few years, we firmly established the mission of the gospel, and people began to come to Christ. I regret, however, I never taught specifically on the Holy Spirit until the very end of my tenure.

If I had the opportunity to lead a local church again, I would follow the model of others in introducing, via dinners or retreats, the teaching of the Holy Spirit. Our friend Pastor Rob Ketterling from the River Valley Church in Minneapolis leads a church of nine thousand people in eight different locations. Rob has successfully used the Alpha Course, a program developed by Nicky Gumbel, who worked for Sandy Millar in London's Brompton Church.

This contemporary Pentecostal church offers multiple services and locations, with no real time for people to linger at an altar, as was the popular method for being baptized in the Holy Spirit in past decades. Thus quarterly, Rob leads a one-day, off-site retreat where his people are given clear, biblical instruction in the baptism in the Holy Spirit, the gifts of the Spirit, and the way this power transforms them into local missionaries for the gospel.

How can you teach your people about the Holy Spirit? If we actually believe what Jesus said—that the Holy Spirit is a gift from the Father and all his gifts are good and if being baptized in the Holy Spirit truly empowers us to be missional—then why would we not teach our people about him?

SPEAK IN TONGUES YOURSELF

When I came to the network office, I was overwhelmed by the magnitude of what was entrusted to me and what Jesus wanted to accomplish. As I began to pray, read, and talk with other leaders about what the next steps might look like, I was taken back to my earlier days of ministry. We were serving in a small town, but we believed God would move in big ways. We launched early morning prayer sessions that seemed to drive us forward. Brenda and I were discussing this recently when she commented, "Those were such rich times of prayer. Words flowed easily from my heart through my mouth, as the Holy Spirit interceded through me for others."

At the network, I knew we needed to focus on prayer first, so I began writing prayers. We launched our Prayer Summit on the first day of business each year, as a first fruit unto the Lord. We also established a network prayer focus with a commitment by the leadership community of area and regional leaders to pray personally for every minister during the year. This prayer focus opened the door to our current Church Planting Initiative and our Revitalization Initiative. I was feeling positive about our decisions.

Sometime during my second year of service, I was driving to work, about a forty-five-minute commute for me. I was thanking Jesus for his goodness to us, grateful for the clear direction. I heard him speak to me in those early hours.

He said, "Don, I want you to begin speaking in tongues regularly each day as you drive to work. I want you to pray in the Spirit as a first fruit to me each day." I was immediately convicted. I had not developed a routine season of prayer in which I prayed in the Spirit. I had let this gift become dormant in my life, and I knew what Jesus was saying to me.

The Scriptures say, "Anyone who speaks in a tongue edifies themselves" (I Cor. 14:4). I knew Jesus wanted to strengthen my inner man for this assignment. I understood speaking in tongues would do just that, so I complied. For the last several years, as I pull out of my garage, I do not listen to the radio or a podcast. I speak in tongues.

The truth is I cannot encourage you to speak in tongues to build yourself up, if I do not pray in the Spirit myself. As a local church pastor, you cannot encourage your church to speak in tongues if you do not as well.

I know some pastors who are reading this cannot believe some Pentecostal pastors do not regularly speak in tongues, but truthfully, some do not. Please hear my heart. Do not beat yourself up, just "fan into flame the gift of God, which is in you through the laying on of my hands" (2 Tim. 1:6). You will, over time, sense your spiritual muscles strengthening, and you will find courage to make critical decisions. You will find clarity as you lead, and you will sense his power in your life. You will find yourself praying for people differently and teaching more effectively.

FINAL WORD

I believe we are on the cusp of something powerful, and the Holy Spirit is leading us into a new day. Each month, the Executive Presbytery invites young leaders to have lunch with us. We let them choose topics, and we ask and answer each other's questions for over an hour. It is a wonderful time.

The most engaging topic for sure is always about the Holy Spirit and his power, and repeatedly we hear the same response. When we talk about healings and miracles and tell stories from our own ministry chapters, these young leaders remark, "We have never experienced this before, and we would love to."

Recently in a session of Turnaround Coaching, I asked the leaders to write down five words they wished described their worship services. One young leader of a thriving, large church responded, "I wish our church were more Spirit-filled." Knowing I would be writing this book, I questioned, "What do you mean?" She replied, "I'm not looking for an emotionally-driven ministry or extremes, just a sense that the Holy Spirit is here, leading us, and empowering us for ministry beyond our normal Sunday experience."

That is my prayer. My heart breaks for our region of seven million people, with 86 percent of them outside a clear understanding of the gospel. Since we are the second largest religious organization in the region, we must take some responsibility for this. Jesus said, "To whom much is given, much is required" (Luke 12:48). It would be just like Jesus to choose the most gospel-resistant area of our nation to launch an awakening. I want to be part of that for sure!

My prayer is the mission of Jesus to reach lost people will captivate our churches, pastors, and missionaries. My prayer is that we will be empowered by the Holy Spirit for this task. My prayer is that we will be both fully missional and completely Pentecostal. Would you join me in this prayer?

Father, we pray that you will imbed the mission of Jesus deeply in our heart. We recognize that when we gave our lives to you, they are no longer our lives, and you can spend them any way you want. We fully give ourselves to the gospel of Jesus for our whole life. We ask you to forgive us if we have let anything become more important in the church we lead, than reaching lost people.

Father, we realize we cannot do what you have asked us to do without the power of the Holy Spirit whom you have provided. We cannot see our people empowered, and we cannot make disciples without his power. We cannot serve our community effectively or release people into ministry without the Holy Spirit's power. We ask you to forgive us if we have tried to do ministry in our own strength, using clever strategies and tactics to avoid asking the Holy Spirit to empower us.

We recognize a day is coming when our work will be tested by fire, and we want to pass the test. We want to build well and to honor your name, Jesus, so we will do as you have asked. We will receive the gift of the Father and will follow him. Thank you for being a good Savior. Thank you for baptizing us in the Holy Spirit and calling us to walk and work with you. We are honored to bring you praise with our lives, as we love you by obeying you. In Jesus' good name we pray. Amen.

Endnotes

Chapter 4:

1   *The Didache* (11:7-8), Christian Classics Ethereal Library, https://www.ccel.org/ccel/richardson/fathers.viii.i.iii.html.

2   "The Martyrdom of Polycarp," p.155 in *Early Christian Fathers*, ed. and trans. Cyril Richardson (New York: Touchstone, 1996).

3   Bernard McGinn, *The Essential Writings of Christian Mysticism* (New York: Random House Modern Library, 2006), xiv.

4   *Luther's Works: Career of the Reformer IV* 43, eds. Lewis William Spitz and Helmut T. Lehman (Chicago: Augsburg Fortress Publishers), 336-7.

5   Extract 26, "Of a letter, from the Rev. Moses Hoge, of Shepherd's Town, to the Rev. Dr. Green, of this city, dated Sept. 10, 1801," in *Surprising Accounts of the Revival of Religion in the United States of America*, ed. William Wallis Woodward (Philadelphia: W.W. Woodard, 1802), 53-4.

6   A. B. Simpson, *The Four-Fold Gospel* (New York: The Christian Alliance Publishing Company, 1890).

Chapter 5:

7   Allan Anderson, *To the Ends of the Earth: Pentecostalism and the Transformation of World Christianity* (New York: Oxford University Press, 2013), 25.

8   Charles F. Parham, *A Voice Crying in the Wilderness*, 4th ed. (Joplin, MO: Joplin Printing Company, 1944; reprint, New York: Garland Publishing, 1985), 31.

9   Frank Bartleman, *Azusa Street*, Reprint (Northridge, CA: Voice Christian Publications, 1962), 51.

10   William Seymour, "The Precious Atonement," *The Apostolic Faith* 1, no. 1 (September 1906): 2.

11   "Good News from Danville, VA," *The Apostolic Faith* 1, no. 1 (September 1906): 4.

12   Allan Anderson, *To the Ends of the Earth: Pentecostalism and the Transformation of World Christianity* (New York: Oxford University Press, 2013), 2.

13   Grant Wacker, *Heaven Below* (Cambridge, MA: Harvard University Press, 2003), 10.

14   Henry Pitney Van Dusen, "The Third Force's Lessons for Others," *Life* (9 June 1958): 122-3.

15   Benjamin Wormald, "Fifteen Largest Protestant Denominations," Pew Research Center's Religion & Public Life Project, May 07, 2015, accessed November 22, 2017, http://www.pewforum.org/2015/05/12/chapter-1-the-changing-religious-composition-of-the-u-s/pr_15-05-12_rls_chapter1-03/.

16   T. M. Johnson, ed., *World Christian Database*, 2010, http://www.worldchristiandatabase.org/wcd/.

Chapter 6:

17   Darrell Guder, *Missional Church: A Vision for the Sending of the Church in North America* (Grand Rapids: Eerdmans, 1998), 3.

18   Alan Hirsch, "Defining Missional," *CT Pastors*, Fall 2008, http://www.christianitytoday.com/pastors/2008/fall/17.20.html, accessed 10 December 2017.

19   Terry Minter, "The Missional Church," *Enrichment Journal Online*, Fall 2012, http://enrichmentjournal.ag.org/201204/201204_EJO_Missional_Church.cfm, accessed 10 December 2017.

20   Ibid.

Chapter 7:

21   https://www.convoyofhope.org/about/

Other Titles by Don Ross

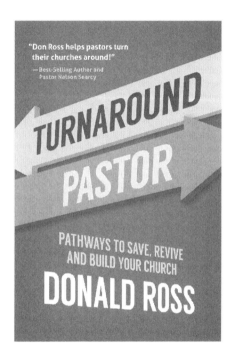

TURNAROUND PASTOR is both a riveting story and a practical guide complete with actionable steps to save, revive, and build your community of faith. Learn from Dr. Ross' personal experience and coaching expertise how to communicate effectively with your congregation, make courageous decisions to move your church forward, lead through major changes, cast meaningful vision, advance Christ's kingdom in your community, and become a Turnaround Pastor.

**Available at www.turnaroundchurch.org
and other Christian book retailers.**

Made in the USA
Monee, IL
22 November 2023

47112031R00094